How to Restore
METAL AUTO
TRIM

Jeff Lilly

MBI Publishing Company

First published in 1997 by MBI Publishing Company, 729 Prospect Avenue, PO Box 1, Osceola, WI 54020-0001 USA

MBI Publishing Company books are also available at discounts in bulk quantity for industrial or sales-promotional use. For details write to Special Sales Manager at Motorbooks International Wholesalers & Distributors, 729 Prospect Avenue, PO Box 1, Osceola, WI 54020-0001 USA.

Library of Congress Cataloging-in-Publication Data
Lilly, Jeff
     How to restore automotive trim/Jeff Lilly.
       p. cm. — (PowerPro)
     Includes index.
     ISBN 0-7603-0331-2 (pbk. : alk.
          paper)
     1. Automobiles—Bodies—Maintenance and repair. 2. Automobiles—Conservation and restoration. 3. Metal-work. I. Title. II. Series: Motorbooks International powerpro series.
     TL255.2.L55   1997
     629.2'62—dc21   97-12211

On the front cover: This 1957 Chevrolet Bel Air Sport Coupe is owned by Lloyd Brekke of Winter Haven, Florida.—*Mike Mueller*

On the back cover: When straightening a dent, there are a few techniques which can be used. A chisel is one tool which works well to tap the edges of the molding back down in the same manner as using a file. Try different tools and techniques to find which works best.

Some basic tools for removal include this SK Tool Co. tool set with WD 40 penetrating oil, Vise grips, wide blade putty knife, screw drivers and a utility knife.

Printed in the United States of America

CONTENTS

TOOLS FOR TRIM REMOVAL

Restoring trim is an interesting and challenging part of the restoration of your classic vehicle. With good tools and the correct techniques, you should be able to accomplish this phase of the restoration on your own.

In the following chapters, we will discuss the steps required for the process. Each section will explain in detail the tools you will need, where to purchase them and how to use them. Any chemicals needed will be discussed with the proper mixture and solutions given. There are special notes and extra tips in each chapter to remind you about certain aspects and to outline some other details that coincide with the overall concept of the chapter.

In the chapter on trim removal, we will discuss a variety of clips that you will encounter while removing your trim. Take special note that each type of clip will be removed in a different way as to do the least amount of damage to the panel and the trim. It is important not to make any extra work for yourself by damaging the moldings during removal.

Once all the pieces are removed it is necessary to clean them, prepare them for straightening, sanding and buffing, and inspecting the pieces to find the damaged areas that will need restoration. There is a special section on removing Flash Chrome from hubcaps and any other pieces that may have been chromed at the factory.

After completing the cleaning process it's time to straighten and reshape the damaged trim. You will learn how to straighten small dents, as well as some advanced techniques for more difficult dent removal.

Keep in mind during this phase of trim restoration that it is best to practice on some unwanted pieces first. This is one of the first steps in which your pieces can be ruined if exact care is not taken. So practice until your confidence and ability are high. This chapter also recognizes that all trim pieces are not flat, straight and easily workable. We also discuss further techniques for restoring odd shaped trim such as concave and convex pieces.

Sanding is the next step, and the book outlines the types of sandpaper to use and how to find and mark flaws as you sand. There is a special section on how to make a setup wheel and how to use it.

After sanding is complete the next step is buffing the stainless for that fine finished product. The chapter highlights the best overall machine to use for buffing and the variety of buffs and their uses. There is also a section on compounds and how to use them. Once again, this is a technique which requires practice, so have some practice pieces prepared.

The last three chapters are diversified techniques which will also sharpen your skills and expand your overall knowledge during the process of restoring your trim.

Some trim pieces need to be reconstructed and welded. The information given in chapter six will help you to accomplish this with ease.

Some trim you will encounter is aluminum. Aluminum is a much softer metal and we will discuss steps for special care. Everything you do to aluminum trim will need to be done slower and with much more caution, because the aluminum is so fragile.

And in the final chapter we will discuss special applications to trim, such as painting inserts, preparation of diecast trim parts, applying copper, nickel and chrome and leveling diecast parts by sanding.

Overall, this book takes you through a step-by-step method for restoring all of the trim on your vehicle, with photos detailing the process.

We recommend that you take your time to read through the entire book first before beginning any of the steps. If you do this, you will have an understanding of the upcoming methods, and why each step is so important.

Trim restoration is not a fast race to the finish, but a quality step in your car's restoration. So prepare yourself by collecting all the supplies and tools you will need beforehand. Order any materials ahead of time and study the book. Once you have completed reading it, you will have a good foundation to begin.

Keep the book handy for reference during the process and outline important factors you will need to keep in mind while restoring. Good luck with your trim restoration. With this book on your workbench and the correct tools—along with practice and patience—you will have the opportunity to complete the restoration on your automobile's trim to perfection.

Trim removal may seem basic, yet it is a critical step in the restoration of an original or classic vehicle. The process must be done correctly to ensure that the trim will not sustain any further damage.

Due to the many different ways the manufacturers installed

You will need some basic tools for removal such as this SK Tool Co. tool set, WD 40 penetrating oil, Vise Grips, wide blade putty knife, screw drivers and a utility knife.

trim, it would be impossible to cover every method, but we shall explain the basics.

Of all damage encountered in restoring trim, one half is usually from improper techniques of removal. This is a combination of using the wrong tools or moldings that were bolted on from behind the panel and prying the molding off before the nut was removed on a hidden clip.

If at all possible, we recommend that you contact a few individuals who are considered authorities on your particular vehicle. One way is to contact a club which specializes in your particular marque. Another is to contact individuals in Hemmings Motor News who are advertising a similar make of vehicle for sale that has been completely restored. Two hours worth of phone calls can save you several hours of restoring damaged trim

which was taken off a classic improperly.

There are specific tools needed for trim removal. You will find that you already own most of these tools around your shop. But if not, look to the manufacturers we suggest for the best quality. Cheaper brands may not do the job as efficiently.

The following list indicates which tools are needed and what the purpose for each tool is. Make sure you gather everything and have it near your working area before beginning any projects.

TOOLS

1. 1/4-inch drive, socket set with 6 point sockets and different extensions including wobble extensions to remove trim from the backside in "hard to reach" places. An SK Tool Co. tool set is perfect for such.

2. WD 40 penetrating oil or any other comparable brand to loosen trim fasteners.

3. Vise Grips of different sizes for clamping and holding clip tabs in place.

4. Wide blade putty knife for prying trim evenly to eliminate damaging trim.

5. Screw drivers, most commonly Phillips head.

6. Utility knife for cutting caulking that has adhered the trim usually found on the front and back windshields during a hobby style repair for leaks caused by hidden rustout.

CHAPTER ONE

CLIPS AND TRIM REMOVAL

Now that you have the proper tools and have spoken with other restorers and collectors, it is time to remove the trim. The more careful you are in removing the trim, the less likely you will damage the back edge or bend any of the pieces.

Before beginning the major portion of trim removal, it is necessary to do some preparation work on the trim clips. Always keep in mind that any damage done to the trim while removing clips and fasteners will add extra hours of work to the pieces of trim.

First you will need to know the basic types of clips and fasteners you will come across to know which method is best for removing a particular type of clip. The following section will list and define how each type of clip was originally installed to help you remove it safely.

There are many varieties of clips, but three are most commonly used. They are the snap-on type, the bolt on type and the spring "V" type. Each type of clip

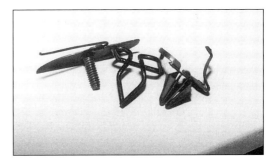

ABOVE AND BELOW: There are many varieties of clips that hold trim to a vehicle. A few of the most common are the Snap-on variety, bolt on variety and the spring "V" variety pictured.

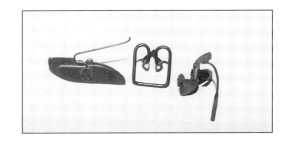

During the process of removing trim always examine the backside of the body panel to identify the type of clip used. This will help you pick the proper method of removal and which tool is needed.

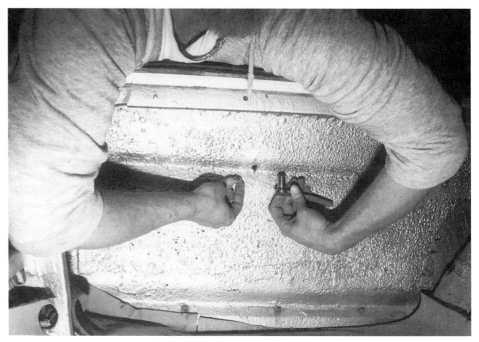

has both a negative and positive aspect, which will be discussed.

It is best to look at the back side of each piece of trim when looking for clips. There may be hidden panels or parts in the way, which makes inspecting the backside more difficult. Often, removing a front fender off the vehicle must be done before a proper diagnosis can be made. This will tell you how the trim was affixed to the vehicle.

In some cases, the factory used snap-on clips that could either be bolted on the car, riveted or snapped in place. The molding snaps over the clip. Other clips are held in place by tension in the form of a prong which protrudes from the clip itself. Often on each end of a door there will be a Phillips screw which holds a clip that slides into the molding. These can be located by looking on the inside by the door striker and between both door hinges.

Remember most moldings are either held on by a snap-on clip or a clip with a stud which protrudes through the panel and is attached by a nut or screw from the back side of the panel. You must examine each molding to determine if it is held on by a snap-on or a clip with a stud that protrudes through the panel, and is attached by a nut or screw from the backside. Examining the molding is the only way to tell what type of attaching clip is used. After the examination, if you are still unsure which type of clip is being used, you might want to call people who are familiar with your vehicle.

Another commonly used clip is the snap-on plastic clip with pin holders which are held on to the vehicle's body metal by protruding fingers forced out by the center pin when pushed through the clip. The molding simply pops on the clip's edges and is held in place. These are found mostly on Chrysler products.

An example of a bolt on clip. They are installed by pushing the clip down on the back of the molding, then twisting so that the outside edges of the clip catch the lip of the molding. A stud is then used with a nut attached for tightening. These are also known as bolt-on variety.

Bolt on clips are installed by pushing the clip down on the back side of the molding and then twisting it so that the outside edges of the clip catch the lip of the molding on the top and bottom. The stud then goes through the panel and a nut attached and tightened.

The spring "V," or wire type of clip style, attaches to the trim by pushing down through an open groove which is on the backside of the molding. Then slide it to the proper location to match the hole in the vehicle's panel. Clips that have a "V" or "X" shaped spring are also used on interior door panel upholstery, although many car makes use them for exterior trim.

Another V-shaped clip has a slightly different base. Some V-shaped clips are attached to the molding differently. They are stuck in and twisted down to catch the clip's edge. A tiny spring wire keeps the tension on the

clips so they will not fall out of the molding while you are aligning the body. The V-shaped prong has a sharper edge which digs into the hole when pushed through the body's metal. This type is very hard to remove, requiring a lot of pressure. This can cause problems to a panel's surface if not approached patiently. We recommend trying to squeeze the prongs from the

An example of the spring "V" or wire type of clip. These clips snap on and off quickly, but tend to either pull the trim piece too tightly, leaving small waves in the body panel, or they fit too loosely with a gap.

The slide-on style clip holds windshield moldings on some 1960s GM cars. Be very careful when removing all window molding clips to prevent chipping the glass.

back side to remove if you can gain access to them.

After all the clips were originally installed by the manufacturer in each section of trim, the trim installer simply turned the molding over, checked the alignment to the body panel and pushed straight down with the point of the "V" centered in the hole. As they were pushed down, the two wires that are crossed forming a "V" shape on the clip's end came together to fit the hole. As it slid through toward the base of the clip, the tapered base end allowed the "V" shape to come back to its original shape and held it tight.

A concern you will have to consider with any "V" shaped clip is that although these are quicker to assemble on the vehicle, depending upon the thickness of paint and/or body filler work in that area, this type tends to either pull the piece of trim into place too tightly. This can leave little,

but noticeable, waves in the body panel from too much tension, or be too loose and the molding will hang with a gap in between the painted surface and edge of the trim. This looks unsightly and may rattle around.

Pinch style clips are held in place by flanges that spread against the inside of the body panel and tighten up as the front side flanges are pinched together with pliers. This holds the clips tight against the body. Then the molding is snapped over the clip, which has holding tabs on the outer edge.

Look out for a combination of clips being used on one piece of trim. Do not take for granted that they are the same.

There are also metal and plastic clips which are riveted to the body and the molding snaps over the edges of the clip. This often results in too much tension with a metal clip, but a plastic clip tends to give and pull to help even out tension so it will not be as tight. This type is most commonly found on rocker panel moldings such as Fords. Rocker panels are almost always bolted on each end and the remainder snap on.

The type of clip with a shoulder that fits in each upper and lower rail of the trim, and a threaded stud which fits through a hole in the body, is the slowest type to assemble. However, these are the best for individual adjusting which aids in preventing damage to the painted surface.

Another consideration is which type of clip was used by the factory for concours restorations when a vehicle will be judged for points. Although other clips would make the fit more accurate, points are won by authenticity, so keep the correct clips even if a molding fits too loosely or tightly if you are doing a concours restoration.

Now that you are aware of the main types of clips and how they are attached, you need to remove and bag them. The following section will demonstrate some of the best strategies for removing the clips and fasteners with the least chance of damaging the trim.

On moldings with "V" style clips, find out where the clip is mounted or pushing through the body. "V" clips have tension which springs out against the hole holding them on. They are usually held either tight or very loose to the body.

Now that you have found the clips, mark the hole on the molding with a black marker. Place a paint stick against the painted section of the car so that you won't ruin the paint, in case the paint job is still good. Using a wide blade putty knife, begin to pry and pop the molding off. The "V" springs should just pop off. But if the clip won't pop off easily try using a pair of pliers and squeezing the "V" together from the back side, pushing slightly so the clip will contract and slide through to the front.

The other type of "V" clips which have the serrated edges catch on the inner edge, and are very difficult to get off. For this clip, you will probably have to use the pliers method so the serrated edges can be squeezed through the hole. Be creative about coming up with strategies for removing stubborn clips without damaging any bodywork, paint, or moldings.

Bolted on clips are usually fine threaded and rusty. This means more threads and more work to remove and clean them, compared to a coarse thread. Remove them carefully to avoid damaging the trim. It is best to begin by spraying all the clips with penetrating oil at least one hour (or preferably overnight) before attempting to remove any pieces. This helps to loosen the clips and break down some of the rust.

Sometimes a threaded stud will turn and round off its square holding shoulder at the base of the clip. This cannot be seen, because it is between the car's body and molding. Case in point why using penetrating oil liberally is even more important!!!

There are a variety of clips that you will come across that are stubborn to remove and will need extra care and attention so that you don't damage the trim or the vehicle. This photo shows a clip which has spun off the molding and now needs to be removed.

To remove this type of clip you must work from the backside. Be sure and use pliers such as Vise Grips to hold the clip from turning.

Using a wide blade putty knife to pry trim off will ensure that no damage will occur to the molding. Always take your time while removing trim, it will save you hours of repair work later on.

On trim clips where threads are too rusty or built up with undercoat, the holding tabs may turn away from the edge on the back of the molding, releasing the hold of the molding. If this happens, remove the molding and then remove the clip afterward by placing Vise Grips on the clip tabs and turning the nut counter clockwise to remove the old clip. This is fine if you don't have to worry about the rotating clip scratching the paint. On a nicely painted car you will want to be sure that the threads are clean, so the clip won't rotate out of the shoulders at the base of the clips.

Bolt on clips need to be removed first by removing the nut on the back side. This will ensure that a molding is not pried off when it is thought to be a snap on clip, when there is really a bolt on type next to it. You would be prying against the tension of the bolt on clip, thus bending your molding.

Always remember to check how the molding is attached from the back side, so you know how to remove it without damaging the trim. If the trim section was held on by all bolt on type clips, then the molding will just pull away once the nuts were removed from all of the studs.

After all bolt on clip/nuts are removed and you have determined that the only other holding clips left are the snap on type, then use a wide blade putty knife to help snap the trim off. Place the putty knife close to or right where the snap on clip is holding onto the vehicles panel. Place a paint stick or plastic spreader under the knife then push down so the putty knife edge does not make contact with the painted surface. This will displace pressure and keep from denting the sheet metal or chipping paint.

Pry down slightly to pop the edge off. If it will not come off use

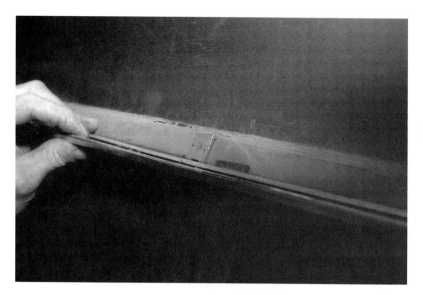

The proper placement of the putty knife using the vehicle's body as a base during the removal of trim. Use a plastic spreader to protect the paint if needed.

Some clips are held on by plastic insert pins. Simply tap them through with a Phillips screw driver to remove them. Retain the pins if you want to reuse them.

Finish removing the plastic snap on clip by tapping the edge of the base lightly with a putty knife. Again keep the plastic centers if you plan on re-using them.

the putty knife by itself and pry up using the vehicle's sheet metal as a base. Unfortunately, this method will tend to leave a scratch in the paint. If you are not going to completely restore the car, then try the plastic spreader method. If you will be restoring the whole car, you need not worry about the old paint.

After you remove the moldings, you will notice some plastic clips that are still attached to the vehicle. These plastic clips have a pressure pin in the center. To remove these plastic clips, simply place a Phillips screwdriver on the pin and tap completely through.

Finish by tapping the edge lightly with a putty knife and removing. Retain the plastic centers if you plan on re-using them.

During removal, make a note as to the condition of the trim's backside edge which makes contact with the painted surface. If it is distorted or uneven, it may crack or gouge out fresh paint work when reinstalled, if not corrected. Further on we will demon-

strate how to restore edges to ensure the molding makes a nice, even contact with the painted surface upon final assembly. Mark these areas where the edges look distorted with a permanent marker after cleanup, so you will remember.

Tips
• Look for a typical slot in the stainless trim where you can easily take the square clips out on all moldings.
• When you encounter rusty brackets on the backside of stain-

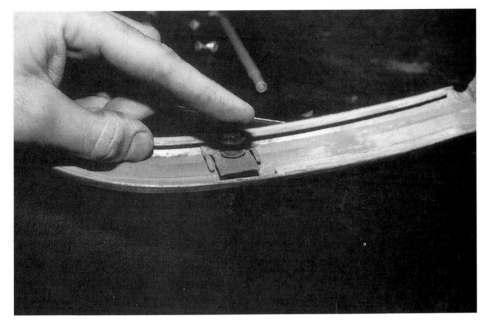

On the backside of trim there is often a series of slots from where the clips are to be removed. By locating and utilizing these slots, clips can easily be installed or removed and slid to the proper position to line up with the holes in the vehicle's body.

less trim, mask off the front side, preferably before or after the part is polished, to keep from scratching it even more.

• Flip the trim piece over. You will see the small bracket that was attached to the stainless. These brackets have a stud on them which goes through the body and help hold the trim in place on the car. These brackets are made of steel and tack welded onto the stainless steel trim. The brackets will rust, so sandblast the bracket and spray stainless steel paint on them.

When removing windshield moldings, use a proper hook tool from an auto supply store or phone order companies such as A & I Supply.

To use the hook, be sure to place it between the bottom of the molding and the top of the glass, without touching the glass. Catch the edge of the snap-clip and the molding will release. This is very critical if you are saving the glass and don't want to crack it.

If there is silicone behind the molding which was used to repair

A bracket on the backside of this trim needs repair. Tape the front side to avoid any more scratches while working the backside.

The backside of the trim which was just taped off shows a small bracket with studs on it. Clean the bracket up, removing rust and painting before starting on the front side cosmetics.

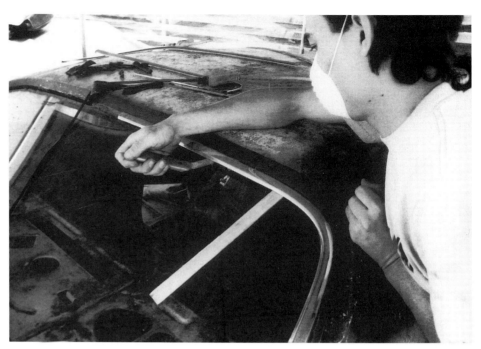

ABOVE AND BELOW: Use a proper hook tool to remove windshield moldings. Place it between the bottom of the molding and catch the edge of the snap-clip, and the molding will release.

leaks, you can cut it with a utility knife. But when a vehicle has had a silicone repair, it becomes much more difficult to catch the clip edge, so be very careful. Do not get impatient, or you may ruin the glass.

It seems that every time you think you have removed all clips and fasteners, there is always one hidden clip remaining which you need to remove. Double check twice! For five minutes of research, it will save you hours of

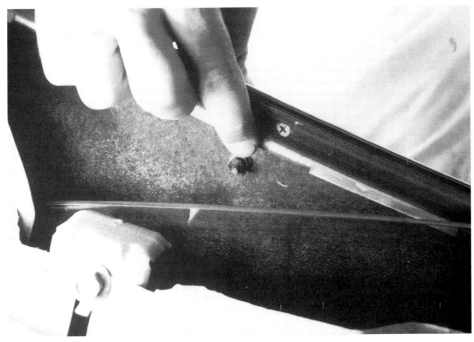

ABOVE AND BELOW: Bolt-on clips are often used to hold on vinyl top moldings where the individual molding sections are connected. This is often a hidden or hard-to-find clip that must be removed before prying the trim off.

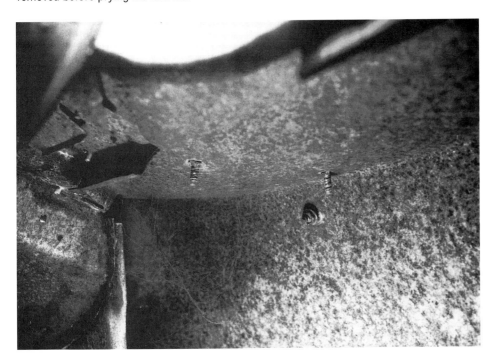

labor, fixing the damage, and of course a couple of Ben Franklin $100 if you have to replace it.

Hidden or hard to find clips must be found and removed to avoid trim damage. Look just inside the rear quarter panel right below the side window glass fuzzies. Another place to look is underneath the trunk ceiling.

Although a diecast stud and thread cutting nut combo is very

Remove the trim with a putty knife. Pry gently while removing trim in case any bolt-on clips are still attached or you will bend the molding under the pressure of prying. Double check for a hidden bolt-on clip if the molding does not want to pop off easily.

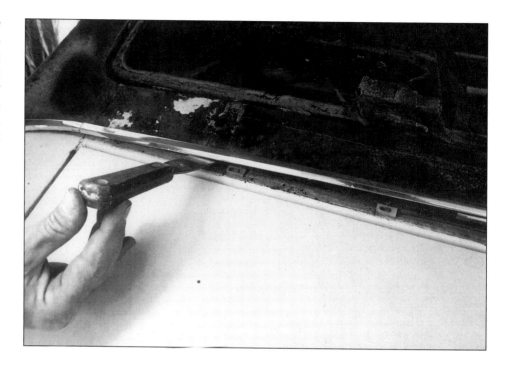

resistant to corrosion, if it has been taken off and reinstalled many times, it cuts a new groove on the stud each time. This tends to strip the existing threads away and ends up not holding very well. Be careful with this type which is made of pot metal and/or a diecast stud.

Some chrome-plated diecast trim pieces have a stud and metal nut. Be sure and check yours before you invest a lot into chrome plating and then find out that you cannot get the nut to tighten up properly when installed!

The factory does not always use the same type of clip on the same trim piece. Some moldings are held on by more than one type of clip, so double check the back side of all moldings.

Even though the molding is snapped off correctly with a wide blade putty knife, any missed bolt-on clips per side will bend the molding, due to the pressure of the putty knife.

Even though you remove one side at a time, do not take for granted that the opposite side is attached in the same manner as the first side. An individual or a body shop may have removed this molding in the past and reattached it with a different

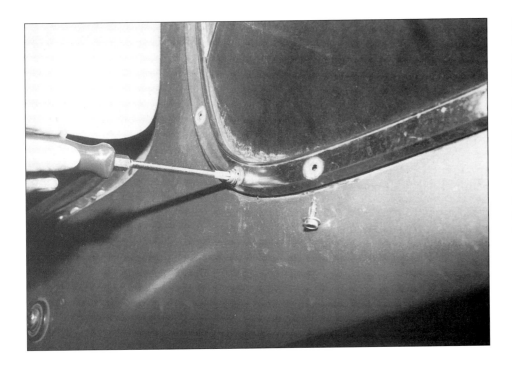

On a convertible at the bottom of the rear window, trim will often have snaps which hold parade boot top covers on. They are often held on by Phillips screws, although the snaps may be attached to the trim by a rivet. If the latter is the case, there has to be a retaining clip underneath the trim. Inspect for these hidden clips. Most of the time you simply slide the trim off toward the front of the car.

clip setup. Once again check the backside!

Trim on a convertible top edge is most generally held on by a Phillips screw which holds the snaps for the top boot cover in place. Other convertible top rails simply slip over the edge with retainer clips that hold it steady while the actual snaps are riveted to the molding itself at the factory.

There are parade boot snaps on convertibles. Try and remove these snap buttons. They will not come off if they are riveted. After you have removed all parade boot snaps (if they do come off) take your thick, wide chisel or putty knife, and hold it against the trim. Then lightly tap on the edge and remove it by sliding it off away from the car toward the interior back seat.

Now that all the different types of clips and fasteners have been removed, and those that were able to be saved are marked and bagged for future use, all the trim should be off of the vehicle. You can now begin to clean, prepare and inspect the trim. If you have clips that were in bad condition, a few sources for new ones are Auveco, Mr. G's or Reproduction Parts Suppliers for your particular vehicle.

CHAPTER TWO

Cleaning and Inspection

Once the stainless and/or aluminum trim has been removed, you will need to clean it to further inspect any damage and to aid in the restoration process. As with anything, the more clean the part is the better to see the imperfections. This also depends upon your vision and ability to critique. If you are going to clean aluminum do not subject it to muriatic acid as described in the following chapter. Read the chapter specified for it.

We will be using different chemicals for different procedures. Each chemical should be treated as the manufacturer recommends on each container. Gloves, goggles, respirators and any other safety equipment should be used whenever possible.

It is also recommended that you use all plastic containers. Pick the best size for your project, and be sure you have cleaned the containers out thoroughly before any cleaning or acid operations are performed.

If you have a very large or long piece of trim you are work-ing, and there is not a sufficient container, simply lay the pieces down on 4-millimeter thick plastic on a floor with the edges rolled up to keep any chemicals from spreading off the plastic. Dispose of all chemicals as per the manufacturer. Disposal recommendations are also made in the following text.

For initial cleanup, do not use a scuff pad on the front side or finish side of the trim. This will dull the finish and will make it hard to find all the imperfections. Use only lacquer thinner to remove road film. Use a razor blade to carefully slice off any stubborn chunks of tar or to remove paint buildup on the edges from production paint jobs. If the front side is extremely dirty with paint over spray, you may use a super fine brass wool pad like those from Eastwood, to clean up the surface. This will keep a decent shine when looking for imperfections later. For now, concentrate on the backside cleanup where it is the dirtiest.

Side moldings are usually filled with years of dirt build up and just need a good cleaning. Use a 3M 7447 scuff pad and a grease cutter such as Dawn dishwashing liquid or Prep Team from 3M. Scrub out the grooves and rinse them with water. A good, stiff hand-held bristle brush also works well.

Other moldings, such as window trim, are often subjected to silicone caulking from repairing leaks around the glass. This caulking becomes embedded into the backside and requires soaking for several hours in naphtha or lacquer thinner to remove efficiently. Once softened, scrape the caulking out with a screwdriver or putty knife. Let it soak more if needed. You can also lay out your moldings on a clean surface and hose them down with water to remove the worst of the dirt before hand cleaning them.

Cleanup

In the following text, we will cover the cleanup process. Read all warnings and safety signs listed on containers of acid, thinner or any chemicals you are using.

For this procedure, we will demonstrate cleanup on a 1957 Chevy hubcap. The same process is used on most trim. This cap has the usual dirt on the backside and must be cleaned using the appropriate cleaners. You will need the right cleaners for the job. We suggest 3M Prep Team and 3M 7447 scuff pads. Dilute the 3M Prep Team five parts water to one part Prep Team. Another good cleaner is Eastwood's Metal Wash (Pt. No. 3500). This concentrated powder is mixed with water to produce up to 2 1/2 gallons of cleaning solution.

To begin, take the diluted 3M Prep Team cleaner and use a 3M 7447 scuff pad and a bucket of water. Clean the front and back side thoroughly. Rinse with clean water. Remember not to scuff the front side or shiny side. Use a soft rag so you will not scratch the surface any more than is already present. Another

The right cleaners 3M Prep Team and 7447 scuff pads will be used in the cleanup procedure on the 1957 Chevrolet hubcap. We have found these to be the best materials, although you may want to experiment with your own solutions.

A hubcap from a 1957 Chevrolet will be used to demonstrate the cleanup process. This cap has the usual type of dirt on the backside that most trim does. It must be cleaned up before any repair work is done.

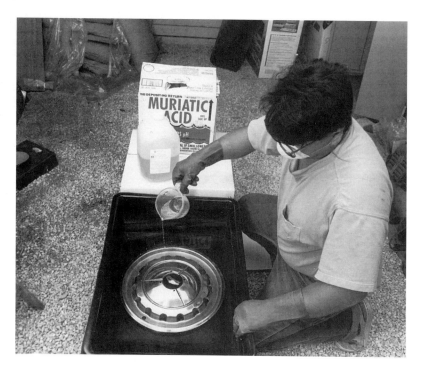

The only way to remove flash chrome is with an acid. Follow the directions in the text exactly. You will be working with muriatic acid and it will need to be neutralized for disposal when you are finished.

effective alternative is *Dawn* dishwashing liquid. The only draw back is *Dawn* tends to foam up quite a bit.

Special prep of stainless such as flash chrome removal is sometimes needed before repairing and polishing can take place. We will show you the techniques to accomplish this. If your parts have no flash chrome you can skip ahead to the inspection section.

Most hubcaps from the factory were flash chromed over the stainless. This must be removed prior to any repairs, sanding or buffing of the stainless. If during sanding and buffing on any piece of trim, you notice a different shade or coloring and can tell you worked through a separate layer of material, this means the part was flash chromed. You must go back and repeat this process to effectively remove the flash chrome. Fortunately, hubcaps usually were the only stainless parts plated. Be aware of this concern though, because you will not

First collect all the supplies you will need. Also, do this project by a water source.

Supplies

The supplies you will need are:
• A five-gallon tub
• Muriatic acid (swimming pool acid) available at your local hardware store
• A half pound of Arm and Hammer Baking Soda to neutralize acid for disposal
• Clean towels

Be sure to wear a respirator and eye shield along with rubber gloves. Depending on the size piece you are trying to remove chrome from, figure on a 3-1 ratio of water to acid.

Directions

1. Fill a tub with three gallons of clean water and place the hubcap or part at the bottom of the tub.

2. Mix in one-half gallon of the muriatic acid.

3. Swirl the mixture lightly, and let it stand a total of 10 to 15 minutes. Be sure and check it every three to four minutes.

4. Agitate the mixture and inspect the chrome removal rate. If the water is warm (85 degrees) the acid will be more aggressive, therefore pull it free from the tub

Checking the part for chrome removal while agitating the mixture every 3-4 minutes is essential. Look for a dull rainbow appearance on the piece. At that time, you will know that the flash chrome has been removed properly.

periodically (five-minute intervals) to check it. When it has a dull rainbow effect, then all the flash chrome is gone. Leave the part in the tub.

5. Take Arm and Hammer Baking Soda and pour one-half pound into the tub. You will notice the bubbling action of the soda while it neutralizes the acid.

6. When the bubbling ceases, remove the hubcap from the tub. This water/acid mix is now neutralized and is safe to pour down your drain.

7. Fill the tub with clean water. Rinse the hubcap by submerging it in this new water.

8. Dry the hubcap with forced air and/or with a clean towel.

After the chrome removal has taken place, Arm and Hammer Baking Soda is used to neutralize the acid mixture into a disposable water ph level. Follow the mixing instructions in chapters 2-5. A bubbling action will occur. Remove the part when the bubbling ceases.

Imperfections show up best in proper lighting. Looking at the piece outside on a cloudy day or in the shade will best reveal imperfections.

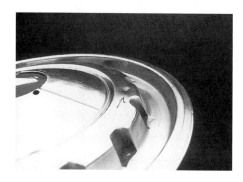

Some imperfections can be seen more readily than others, due to their severity and size. Make sure to locate even the most minute imperfections.

be able to polish the stainless effectively with the layer of chrome still on the part.

You will want to remove the flash chrome with acid. Be sure to follow the directions very specifically.

Now that you have your trim pieces all cleaned up, it is time to

inspect them for damage and scratches that need work. A major factor that will help you is inspecting these pieces in correct lighting. If you have a glare of any type on the stainless, you may not notice some flaws.

Looking at the piece on a cloudy day or in the shade is the best situation to perform this step. Never do this in the bright sunlight.

On a flat surface such as a table, look down the length of the molding or trim piece and mark all apparent dents or irregular waves you want removed with a permanent black marker in the form of a circle, or color the whole dent. The permanent marker will help to find high and low areas during the repairing stage.

Another good way to find imperfections, especially if you do not have a critical eye for finding flaws, is to use a 6-to 9-inch long hard block. Get 400 grit wet sandpaper with a bucket of water, and sand on a sideways

As you locate the flaws on each trim part, mark them with a permanent black marker. Circle the area or color in the whole dent. When you sand them down, any marker that is left will indicate areas that still have some flaw or imperfection in them.

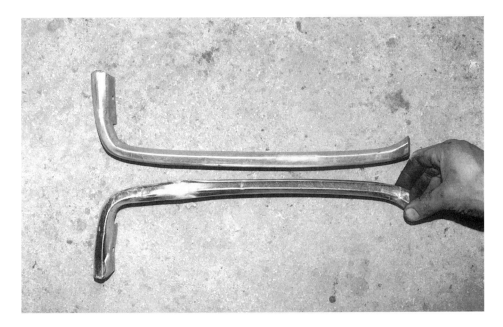

When ordering a piece from a salvage yard, it is best to take a photo of the damaged piece laying next to the good piece from the opposite side of the car so that the salvage yard knows exactly what to send. Do not use a flash on your camera, or you might get a glare off the stainless. Take pictures in shade or on a cloudy day.

pattern. (This will allow the low spots to remain shiny and the flat undamaged areas to be scratched from the blocking). It is still a good idea to use the permanent marker on these areas once you have located them.

At this point, it may be wise to set aside any pieces of trim that have a lot of damage, and find better ones if there is such a piece available. This may be a more efficient use of your labor time.

It's important to tackle the small damaged parts and become more familiar and more confident in your abilities to restore trim to your liking, before you can move on to a heavily damaged part.

If you do decide to replace the part, it is best to photograph each piece and send copies of the pictures to salvage yards. This way there will be no mistakes and you will receive the correct part for your vehicle.

Most trim parts are shiny. Therefore, a camera with a flash will cause a glare on the film. Your best photo will be achieved outside on a cloudy day with the part laying down on a gray or tan background. Lay its undamaged twin from the other side of your classic next to it, if it is available. Make sure the part is cleaned up in order to get a good photo, and shoot the picture using no flash. Tell the salvage yard whether it is the passenger or driver side you are in need of.

Also, be sure to keep in mind how the trim originally fit to the painted surface or body of your project. You may need to photograph the piece held in place, so you can recall later how it needs to be installed.

Of course, a new piece may not fit perfectly. You will learn how to make changes to correct this by filing and sanding to fit the piece to the painted surface later in the straightening chapter.

Your trim has now been removed from the vehicle correctly. A good cleaning has been done, the parts are inspected, and damaged areas marked. Move on to the straightening method in Chapter 3.

Tools that you will need for the straightening process include: various hammers, different shaped super fine hand files, chisels, dental picks, punches and pliers.

CHAPTER THREE

STRAIGHTENING DENTS

This chapter will demonstrate the artistic techniques that really make the difference in restoring automotive trim. Go through the steps slowly until you improve. For the most part, the basic process involves removing dents with a circling motion, starting at the outside perimeter of the damage and working your way into the center.

Long, thin moldings require extra work, because they need to fit the body of the vehicle by adjusting the backside edges which make contact with the paint. To achieve this, you may need to twist the moldings slightly and use a block of wood to press down on the edge for uniform movement. When sighting down the side of the molding, look for an even contact to the painted surface.

This chapter will also discuss using files—which techniques to

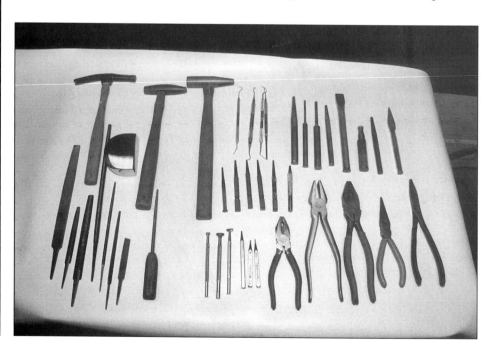

use and how much pressure to apply. Other techniques covered include how to sand each piece to remove file marks, and how to ready each piece for polishing.

As in any of the preceding steps, have your tools out and ready. The tools you will need for this aspect of the project are:

TOOLS

1. **Various small hammers**
2. **Fine grade hand files of different shapes**
3. **Chisels**
4. **Dental Picks**
5. **Punches with various levels of sharpness at the tips (at least one dolly)**
6. **Pliers (Channel Lock has the best selection of sizes.)**

Tips on Files

• Nicholson files are sold by Sears and have a lifetime warranty.

• Obtain a small brass wire brush to clean the metal chips off of the files during use.

• Purchase only fine grit tooth files. The intent is to only shave down small amounts of metal at a time to level out the surface.

Now we will begin the steps for straightening. Again, remember to start out with smaller, less severely damaged parts, and work your way up to the worst pieces. You should start by practicing on some scrap pieces which won't go back on the vehicle. Eastwood's Mini Anvil and Trim Hammer (Pt. No. 1486) are handy tools. The hammer has a 4-ounce head and both tools are the right size for removing many trim dents.

To begin with, we will show how to tap out small dents. Although we are performing the task on a hubcap, the basic technique is the same for all stainless and aluminum trim. The only big difference is that if the part is flimsy, you will have to support it with an appropriate block of wood or metal to keep it from bending while working on it. On long pieces, try taping them down with 2-inch tape in a few areas to secure them while working. Flip the hubcap or part over and place the dented area on a 1 x 4 piece of smooth wood. Using a round 1/8-1/4 diameter overall punch with a rounded tip, start tapping lightly and then harder if needed. Experiment with your style on an old part first to get used to the right amount of tapping pressure.

Do not use a sharp pointed tip, or you will straighten too much, and perhaps puncture the stainless, making a hole in the metal.

Starting on the outer edge, tap lightly, going around the dent clockwise. When you have made a complete circle, work in toward the center, tapping a small por-

Tapping out dents on stainless is done with a circling technique. Tapping lightly with a round punch works well to start with. You may have to support longer pieces with a wood block. Outside lines can be worked out with chisels. You will find that grinding your chisels and punches to your desired points and thickness will give you optimum results. Make them fit your application.

After tapping the stainless, file across the once dented area with a hand file 10 strokes at a time before inspection. Use a file that is 1/2 to 1-inch wide or narrower if the dent is smaller. Only file forward and not on the back stroke or you will dull the file.

tion at a time (1/32 to 1/16 of an inch) and repeat the circle process.

After you have worked the dent out and have finished your initial tapping, flip the hubcap back over. Using light finger pressure, take a hand file that is close to the width of the dent, or at least half as wide, and slice going forward only. Start with 10 strokes of cutting and make a note to yourself which way the cutting teeth are on the file.

A file cuts only one way. Do not apply pressure while pulling back or you will dull the file. It is a good idea to purchase a small brass wire brush from a hardware store. Use this to clean the metal residue from the file every now and then. This will ensure a clean, even cut. The permanent marker that is left will indicate any low areas that are still apparent.

If you can remove the remaining marker left on the surface with a few more strokes, then do so. But if it takes any more strokes than that stop, or you

may cut the surface too thin and eventually go through the steel, which will ruin the part.

We highly recommend that you experiment with an old piece to get acquainted with your own style of tapping and filing. Remember, practice makes perfect.

After the initial filings you will see that there is only one small dot left, an area the size of a pinhead that still needs to be tapped out.

Simply flip the part over one more time and lightly tap right on the spot where the marker shows the pin spot. Then file one to two more strokes until it is gone. After this is tapped and file finished, proceed to the next step.

Sometimes, if your piece is damaged beyond repair, it is better to buy other ones in better shape, because they will take too much time to repair, from an efficiency standpoint. There are some pieces that you may not be able to obtain, and you will have to repair them. In this short chapter, we will show

Any of the permanent black marker left after the filing process indicates small imperfections are still left in the stainless which need further work to get out.

you a few advanced techniques to achieve this.

One method is called "Edges First." Remember, when you want to straighten a piece of trim, the main thing to be concerned with is first working on the edges of the molding that make contact with the painted surface.

If the edges need no work, then proceed to any edges in the center of the molding. After these edges are completed, proceed to the body of the molding to straighten any other irregularities, using the "marker circling method" discussed earlier.

The edges first method takes the stress out of the molding and allows for room in the body of the part to move.

Of course, the types of damage you will come across are as various as the type of car marque you choose to work on. So, we have selected a few types of parts to demonstrate some of the steps that you can use on similar parts.

Windshield

On some windshield parts, if you pry on the molding during

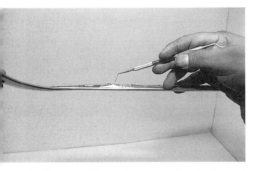

On bent or twisted trim, determine the type of damage on the molding so you will be able to determine the best steps to use to straighten it. This can be done by sighting the part and marking the damage. You should practice on a rough discarded piece first.

disassembly, it can bend. So, it is very important to remove it carefully and not to bend the piece even more.

The first step after cleaning is to turn over the molding, placing the front side down on a level surface or 1x4 piece of hardwood. Carefully pry back the lip just enough to gain access to the inside of the molding's edge with wide-nose pliers.

Use the permanent marker method to highlight the damaged area. Take a 1/2-to 1-inch-wide chisel that has a blade which has been rounded, to match the corner of the molding edge. Lightly tap out the very outside edges to make them level and straight. Sometimes having an assistant to hold the part on the right angle can really help to tap the exact area.

Be sure to use a 1x4-inch board under the part being worked on for support. This will let it give slightly with each single tap, which will release the dent carefully.

Pry back the edge of the molding to expose the damage. Use as wide a pair of pliers as possible to keep any twisting of the metal to a minimum. Pry back the lip just enough so that a chisel can fit inside.

Before working on the body, it is best to straighten the outside lines of the trim first. Using a 1/2- to 1-inch wide chisel with a rounded blade, tap out the very outside lines of the trim to make them straight.

After the edges are finished, begin work on the body. Little, tiny spots that are stubborn can be removed with a slightly pointed punch when tapped very easily. For the center of the molding, repeat the circling method of tapping from the outer perimeter into the center of the dent.

Once the outside edges are satisfactory and you have filed the front side at least one time near the very edges, check to be sure you have enough room to work the backside more near the edges if needed. Especially check the area the lip will cover when it is

When tapping out the body of the trim it is best to use a circular tapping method working from the outer perimeter into the center of the dent. Practice is the only way to know how much hammer pressure you should apply with each tap.

Finish the body or center from the back side with a small hammer such as one used in upholstery work. This works best on any irregularities which may not have been satisfactorily removed with the circular tapping method.

tapped back down in its proper place. Finish any irregularities with a small hammer such as the type used in upholstery.

Now turn the piece over and file the molding smooth. Be careful not to shave the metal too thin. Use a very fine tooth file for best results. If during the filing process you find a spot that is too low, flip the piece back over and tap out the spot more.

If you have the edges to a satisfactory stage, lay the molding front side down on a flat steel surface. Tap the edge back over

File the molding smooth while checking for highs and lows, determined by the amount of marker that is left. If the area is still too low, flip it over and tap out the spot more. Remember, 10 strokes with the file is enough to tell if you have tapped out the right areas.

Using a square hammer to bring edges back down in place assures you that the edge will be smooth and even, so that it will have an even contact on the painted surface or glass.

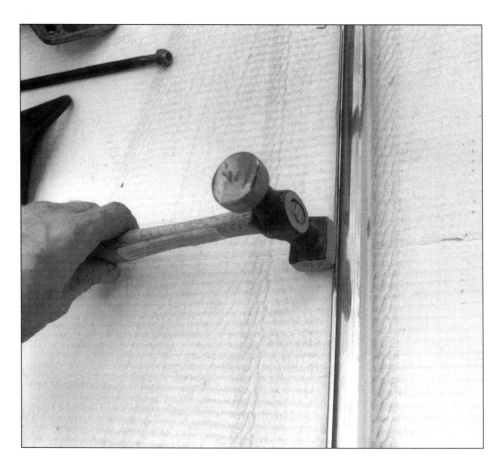

where it belongs, being sure it is even and smooth so it will make an even contact with glass or, as in the case of a door molding, even contact on a painted surface.

If you are a beginner, have a helper steady the trim while you hold a slapping spoon, two to three-inch wide chisel or putty knife against the lip to tap the edge back down.

This method will move the edge back down evenly without the worry of uneven contact by using the hammer by itself. Also, cut a paint stick to fit in between the edge lip and the molding for support, so you will not tap the trim too far down.

Flip the trim to the front side again and file it until it is level. Remember the metal is very

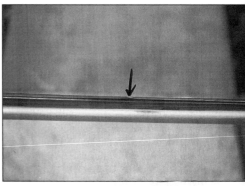

A dip on the molding's backside may press up against the finished paint and crack it when it is attached to the body. Double check the backside edges of all pieces before you attach them and straighten any dips you find.

thin, so only file five to ten strokes, then check it so you don't make it too thin.

There is an arrow pointing toward a dip on the backside edge in a finished molding. This dip, if it is not straightened, will press up against finished paint and crack it when attached to the body. Make sure you examine all the edges on your finished trim before assembly. To fix the dip, place two-inch Norton Blue Line tape on the clean polished side of the trim. Now, lay the taped side down on a piece of cardboard which should be resting on a solid bench. Take a squared hammer and tap with just enough pressure on the edge of the trim to get the high point down, or try the spoon tapping method.

For the most part, you will encounter the basic style moldings that are long and flat on the sides of most autos and trucks. Every so often you will encounter odd shapes such as concave or convex moldings. These types of moldings take

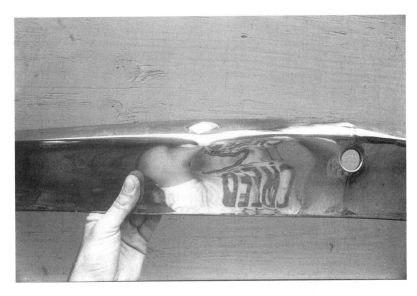

special dollies to straighten and are not as easy to achieve perfection as the flat style.

Using the basic techniques discussed next will help you overcome any fear you have of these special application trim pieces. As we have mentioned before, try to experiment with a used piece of trim if this is your

This picture shows several dents in a convex/concave shaped piece of trim. This is a lot harder than what you have tackled so far. Follow the techniques we will show. Practice makes perfect, so try some old parts first if needed.

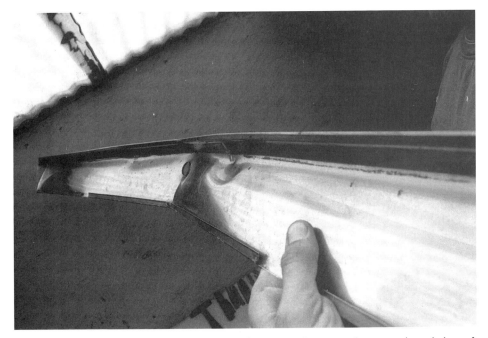

Viewing from another angle will show different damage on the convex/concave shaped piece of trim. Different angle viewings are needed to give you a more accurate idea of how to approach the damage.

To begin the repair work, you will want to start with the longest lines, first then move to the shorter ones. So work on the outside lines first. Follow the steps as described in the text.

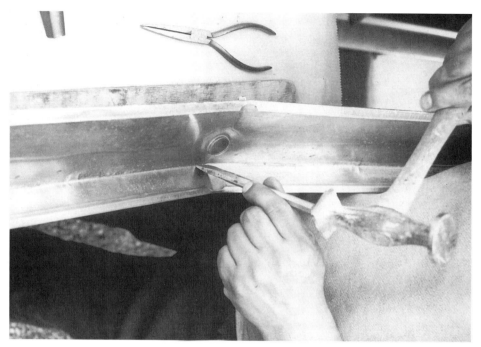

first time restoring an odd-shaped piece.

Odd shapes are concave or oval convex moldings used on various areas of a vehicle. They are found on almost every manufacturer's vehicles at sometime or another. We will show you how to straighten these different style moldings. These moldings have many shapes and contours that can be removed easily with a little common sense.

To begin the repair work turn the piece over on a 1x4 smooth sided piece of wood. Now take a 1/2-inch wide blade chisel with a rounded edge or blade end and place it in the crease starting on one side of the dented area.

Always straighten outer edges first as you did with the long flat moldings. Move down a quarter of an inch at a time until you have covered the crease the whole length of the dented area.

When this is complete, take a 3/8- or a 1/4-inch wide blade chisel

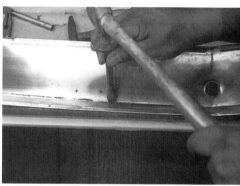

Increase the sharpness of the line by taking a 3/8- or a 1/4-inch wide blade chisel with a slightly sharper edge. Tap lightly. Move down the line half the width of the chisel you're using each time you tap.

The middle vertical crease is second to be repaired. Use a 1/2-inch wide blade and tap in the opposite direction.

with a little sharper edge and tap lightly the same way described to give the crease a crisp line.

The middle vertical crease is second, so use your 1/2-inch-wide blade and tap the opposite direction if your situation warrants. Always start with the longest lines first, then move onto the shorter ones.

Now take a thick flat chisel and tap starting on one end and working your way to the other end of the damage on the top flat portion of the molding.

If there are any small imperfections tap them lightly with a small rounded or flat punch to release the high area. Move around in a circular motion.

A thick flat chisel is used to tap with on the top flat portion of the molding. Start on one end and work your way to the other end of the molding.

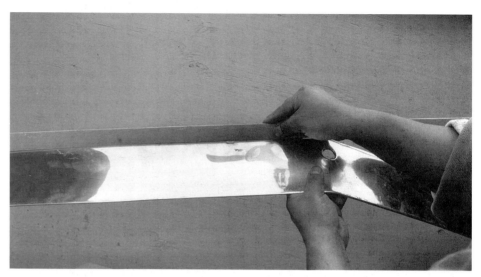

Always rely on your straight edge to check your work for accuracy. This is the only way to really determine how straight the piece is.

Using a small, round, pointed chisel to tap, and moving in a circular motion is the best way to remove small imperfections.

Next take a straight edge and see how true the line is that you have straightened. Make any adjustment you may need by repeating the steps outlined before.

Next we will discuss the repairs on the large contoured areas. After you are satisfied with the edges, proceed to the contoured area using a contoured dolly. Be sure to pick the dolly that fits the molding best.

Place the dolly directly on the low dented side which is the out-

side or finished side you see when looking at your vehicle. Tap lightly on the back side.

Start around the outside perimeter and encircle the dent until you have worked in to the center.

Patience is needed to achieve quality. If you do not proceed carefully and slowly, you will damage more than you will fix. Relax and do the job right and achieve the level which you are capable.

Take your permanent black marker and mark the whole area which was damaged on the outside. Then take a contoured sanding block, available from Hutchins, or a piece of PVC plastic water pipe which fits best in the contour; PVC is available in 1/2, 3/4, 1, 1-1/2, 2-inch sizes and larger. Use 220 grit wet and dry paper to sand with a cross-hatching direction. You will be able to see where your high and low spots are when you do this.

The concave trim was darkened with a marker before it was

To repair large contoured areas, use the dolly and tap method. Place the dolly on the low dented side and tap lightly on the backside, starting at the outside perimeter and encircling the dent until you have worked in to the center.

A closeup angle of how your dolly should fit. We are using the dolly and tap method as explained before, a circular motion. Use patience and more patience. Your tapping pressure must be consistent.

When you use 220 grit wet sandpaper with water in a crisscross pattern, you will be able to see your high and low spots most effectively. Use a flat or PVC pipe sanding block—whichever fits your part.

sanded to show you where the highs and lows are. You will need to tap the dark areas more from the backside and repeat the procedure as discussed previously.

As you would expect, if the dark marker area is still visible but has been scuffed with the sandpaper slightly, then it is probably not a very deep, low spot. If the marked area has not been touched with the sandpaper at all, then it is a deeper dent. You will need to tap a little harder on the deeper dents from the back-side.

Continue sanding the area every time you tap a section to see if you are tapping with the right pressure and in the correct areas. Continue to sand the darkened front side every time a series of tappings has been performed.

When all marker spots are gone, the metal work is finished and it is ready for polishing.

Straightening

The following will discuss the straightening technique for long, thin moldings that are bent or twisted. In our example, the upper molding is bent while the lower twin remains in its original form.

After turning the molding around, you can see the edge is very uneven from damage that occurred during disassembly. This damage was inflicted from a screwdriver prying on it when the clips were still holding it down.

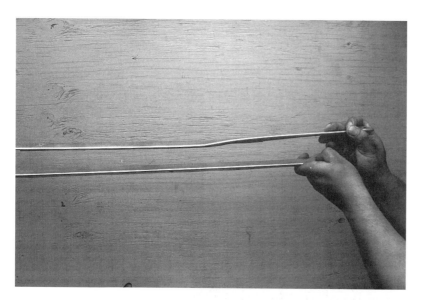

A bent upper molding which needs to be straightened using the techniques for long, thin moldings which are bent or twisted.

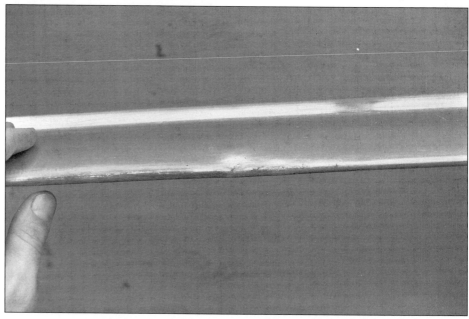

On this long, thin molding, you can see that the damage was caused by prying up with a screwdriver while the clips were still attached. Had the proper inspection procedure been followed as specified in Chapter 1, this would not have occurred.

Aluminum moldings tend to get dipped in from the backside when using a screwdriver to pry off instead of a putty knife as explained in chapter 1. If this goes undetected, it can cause uneven pressure on the painted surface. This can eventually lead to paint chipping or a warped body panel when assembled to the vehicle.

The person responsible for this damage did not check for fastening clips when they were trying to remove the molding.

On the same molding, there is an area that is dipped in from the backside which, if undetected, will often put uneven pressure on the painted surface and can lead to many problems including warped body panels and/or chipping of paint upon tightening. This is usually from a dent on the outer finished side and seems to happen on aluminum moldings more often then the stainless variety. Because aluminum is a softer metal, the trim seems to

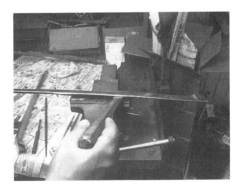

We use PVC pipe to ship out long moldings for comparison and purchases from salvage yards. It is a safe way to keep your pieces from getting bent and damaged. You can buy this pipe from a hardware store. Get the PVC cut as long as the longest piece you will be sending, then pack newspaper in the ends so that they won't be shifting around inside the tube. Finish the packing with PVC end caps taped on both ends.

On long, thin moldings you can use a vise to tweak and or twist the edges back to shape. Make sure you have rubber or aluminum jaws on the vise or put tape on them to keep from scarring the trim.

To fix dents in flat surfaces, you need to pull back the edges of the trim with wide blade Vise Grips so that the flat surfaces and inside lines are exposed completely.

give more throughout the whole range of the metal.

If you need to send out long strips of molding to compare them or are buying long moldings from out of state, buy some long PVC tubing from the hardware store. Put capped ends on the tub-

ing and stuff newspaper inside both ends so moldings won't be damaged during shipping.

You can also use a vise to help in the edge straightening process for long thin twisted moldings. First, you need to either tape the vise jaws or purchase rubber or alu-

After you have pulled back the edges of your trim. Use a 3/4 wide flat chisel for straightening the flat areas and lines. Tap out the inside line starting on one end and working down the length of the damaged area. Move down the line 1/2 inch at a time.

minum jaws to prevent scarring the trim piece. Eastwood carries a supply of various jaws. Next, place the damaged molding in a vise and lightly tighten one edge into a taped jaw. With a wide-blade chisel, pry up on the edge to achieve a uniform height across the entire length, thus straightening the trim in the process. You will have to move the molding from one end to the other to achieve this. The trick is holding the other end with your hand while prying. Be gentle while experimenting.

If the trim is dipped instead of higher, like our example, then reverse the way you have placed the trim in the vise and go downward instead of upward.

If there are dents such as door dings in the flat surfaces, turn the molding over and with a flat tipped pair of Vise Grips, pull back the edge to expose the flat surface of the molding.

Vise Grip pliers come in many sizes and types which work well for trim restoration. Because of the wide gripping area, this particular style of Vise Grip does not bend the metal in a wavy fashion, which allows the metal to go back into place after restoring the very important front side.

In a tight, confined area, you will not be able to use these wide-style pliers. It would be better to use a pair that has a narrow tip until you pull back the damage, and then use the wide ones to finish.

To use a wide chisel for edge straightening, place a 3/4-wide chisel—always edges first—and tap out the edge starting on one end, working down the length of the damaged area. The same size

A 3/4 wide chisel can also work on small damaged flat surface areas if you hold the chisel on the right angle. Remember, tapping pressure is very important. Practice and follow the techniques as described in the text for this.

chisel works well to get tiny damaged areas straightened. Use a smaller chisel to tap out any little imperfections as you look the piece over. Remember, chisels should not be sharp on the ends, just level for even contact.

Once you have tapped the areas down, marked and lightly sanded the front side, and are satisfied with the straightening on at least the outer edges, turn the molding back over. Lay a flat file, steel strap or a paint stick down on the inside of the trim. Then tap the edge back down for accuracy.

If necessary, use a permanent marker and repeat the block sanding technique for finding highs and lows. The purpose for reinforcing the edge when tapping it back down is to provide stability, so that the edge will go back in place in a mild, uniform way and the metal does not get distorted.

There is another method for flattening down the edge. When you are satisfied with the top side, turn the piece back over and place a thick chisel that fits in between a portion of the molding which was never altered. Slide the chisel down to the starting point, where you pulled the lip back to straighten. Start tapping down the edge or lip with your hammer, and gradually move down toward the other end.

Once you have done your best on straightening the outer edges and flat surfaces, you need to file the front side. When you have obtained the best results, you can turn the molding over front side down and lay a file inside the trim against the outer edge which was just repaired. Tap on this to get the edges back down to the factory height.

Choose the method which is most comfortable for best results. A square end hammer works well. A slapping spoon about 2-1/2-inch wide placed on the trim first and then tapped with a hammer also yields good results. The spoon is already in the correct position, so you will eliminate missing the spot with a hammer.

Finally, compare the part for uniformity by placing a straight edge beside the repaired area. If the part is meant to be straight, you should not see more light in any one area then the next.

If you are not sure how straight the molding is supposed to be, look at the matching piece on the opposite side of the vehicle. If that piece is undamaged, you can determine the correct contour.

A chisel can also be used to tap the edges of the molding back down in the same
manner as you used the file. Try each technique to find which you like best.

Place a straight edge beside the repaired area of the trim. This way you can check the accuracy to be sure your repair was optimum.

CHAPTER FOUR

MARKING AND SANDING FLAWS

One of the most important steps in your stainless repair is sanding. In this chapter, we will discuss specialized techniques for sanding different types of trim. To begin, you need the tools necessary for completing the process.

Stainless steel is so hard to cut, that it takes abrasives and high speed to cut it efficiently. Pictured are the types of sanders and grades of sand paper that will be used aside from the last stage of hand sanding. Some of the abrasives and tools necessary include:

1. Dual action sander from National Detroit with a 6-inch pad. A 3-inch pad is also useful.

2. 80 grit DA paper used for very stubborn scratches or small dings. Be careful with this abrasive, because this grit grade can

There are many sandpapers, flap wheels and different tools to use when cutting stainless. Some are a Die Grinder for flap wheels and a Dual Action Sander with a 6-inch pad. The best grits of sandpaper to use are 80 grit, 180 grit and 320 grit D-A paper. If you can afford to purchase both the Die Grinder and Dual Action Sander, do.

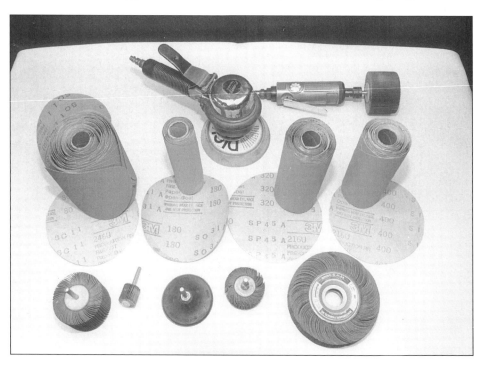

cut through stainless metal very quickly if not monitored. Practice on an old part.

3. 180 grit DA paper used to smooth out minor irregularities such as scratches you can almost feel with a fingernail, small pits and file marks or scratches.

4. 320 grit DA paper and 400 grit are used to sand out very fine scratches that would otherwise take too much time for the Sisal buffing wheel to remove.

5. Flap wheels for sanding and grinding out imperfections in hard to get areas or small moldings which we will discuss in greater detail later.

6. DA stands for the Dual Action model sander. Always set the sander on grinder mode. This means that the sanding disc will make a complete circle, not the orbital feathering motion. There are many companies which sell a DA sander ranging in price from $25 to $200 and above.

Before you proceed to sand your project pieces, take old pieces of stainless and experiment with the different grades of paper so that you will see how quickly each grit cuts the metal. This will help you to determine which paper to use on the area you just filed, and how much pressure to apply. Try to keep the air pressure on your DA to 60 psi and set the sander on the cutting mode, not the orbital. Push the button in and lock the cam so a grinding, clockwise rotation takes place.

Another tool you may want to experiment with is the Expander Wheel by Eastwood. This tool conforms to contoured pieces

and leaves a smooth surface. Different grits can be used with this tool as well.

For fine polishing Eastwood's range of 3-M™ Trizact™ bands work great and save time. The unique pyramid structure of the abrasive assures uniform cutting

Eastwood's Trizact bands work great for leveling defects in flat or slightly curved areas, and since they're available in a wide range of grits from 200-1200. You can go right from the 1200 grit band to final buffing!

Eastwood sells this Expander Wheel which conforms to the contours of different pieces and leaves a smooth surface. You can use different grits for a variety of finishes.

action. In other words an old band cuts almost as well as a new band. These bands won't load up like regular abrasives will when you're working with aluminum because they're self lubricating. It is best, however, to use a little tripoli compound on the A-30 (200 grit) or A-16 (1200 grit) band as a lubricant for best results.

After the surface is smooth, all that's needed is final buffing with white rouge on a loose buff. The part comes up to a mirror shine in seconds. In our example, we will be using the hubcap we cleaned and straightened the dents from the previous chapters.

Take the DA sander and begin with 80-180 grit, working your way up to 320 and then 400 grit paper to smooth out the area that was just filed. How well your piece was straightened and how much pressure you apply, will determine the grade of paper you should use and how much time spent with each grit.

Be extremely careful with 80 grit, or you may ruin the part by sanding too thin or warping the part from too much heat. When you see the marks or scratches are

The DA sander must be used with the correct angle so that a piece does not get ruined by being sanded or filed through. The DA is a versatile tool. Be extra careful with 80 and 180 grit paper, they are very aggressive.

gone, switch to the next grit higher until you reach 400 grit.

It is very important to experiment slowly and remember to stay off the corners and edges, since they will file and sand through much faster than the flatter areas. We cannot emphasize this point enough! It is very easy to cut through edges and

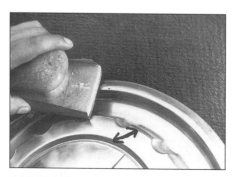

ABOVE AND RIGHT: Hand blocking final scratches for an ultra smooth finish with 400-600 grit wet paper and water is the ultimate. Always sand in a criss-cross pattern.

corners and ruin a piece of trim, so be very careful.

At this point, for best results, get a hand block and 600 grit wet sandpaper ready with a fresh clean bucket of water. Keep the sandpaper wet and sand in a criss-cross pattern. Block the areas in opposite directions. This will make the metal "ripple-free" and produce excellent metal, ready for shine polishing. Use an "XXX" pattern only. Also, color the area to be sanded with a marker to see the high/low areas.

Note that there is always the chance of making the part too thin with high-speed sanders. This is true especially if the trim was already fixed in that area once before incorrectly, or it is a particularly delicate part.

There is an excellent way to achieve quality results and greatly reduce the chance of taking the part too thin after the filing process. Take 220 grit wet sandpaper, water and a hard block. Sand the piece until you smooth out all the file marks. Then go ahead and DA or hand sand with 320-400 grit and continue on to buffing.

It's important to be able to recognize slight flaws in order to fix them. We will discuss some signs to look for in finding flaws and small dents. Once you locate flaws and begin to level them, the flaws will lessen. However, every time you use a finer grit, you will find a different level or size of flaw. The obvious flaws disappear, and the flaws that are difficult to see become apparent. Yet the obscure flaws are tiny in comparison to the ones first located. As indicated in earlier chapters, using a black marker on imperfections helps make them apparent so they can be worked out. For the following procedures, mark the piece in one direction,

Special hand sanding techniques help to keep you from filing the part too thin. Using 220 grit wet sandpaper, water and a hard block, sand until all the file marks are gone. Now DA or hand sand with a 320-400 grit paper and water.

Mark the flaws with an arrow going in the direction of the flaw. Sand in the opposite direction of the arrow you marked for the best results.

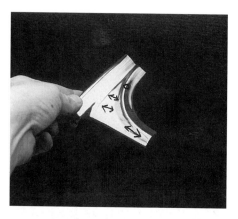

but sand in the opposite direction for best results.

You may encounter inconsistencies in the stainless, such as a groove in the metal after straightening or unsightly factory press lines which you may want removed. Draw an arrow in the direction the inconsistency travels and sand in the opposite direction of the mark for optimum results.

Also, circle the pits in the stainless which you are unhappy with, so you can remove them. It is important to look the part over from many angles. Mark flaws in the direction they appear, then work them the opposite direc-

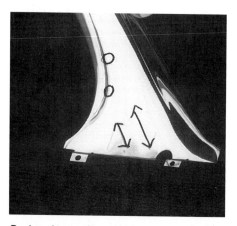

During inspection, for optimum results mark pits and scratches in diffused or shaded light. Then work them out by sanding in the opposite direction that you marked.

tion. Remember, always inspect and mark flaws in diffused or shaded light for the best visibility. This is the same technique used to do any bodywork on a car. Cross sanding makes a panel uniform. Always sand in a cross direction, devoting the same amount of time to each side.

In some examples there are imperfections around the contoured edge. These are called 'Big

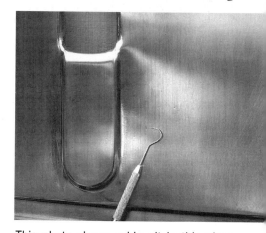

This photo shows a big pit in this piece near the dental pick. These need to be sanded out with the 220 DA or a 320 grit for optimum results.

Pits.' This type of flaw should be sanded out with 220 DA or a 320 grit, depending on your comfort level. Then use 600-800 grit wet paper, sanding by hand. You may need to review the buffing steps on pieces which are to be considered show quality.

Analyze each part several times to find flaws, and mark each one you wish to work out, depending on the quality level you wish to achieve. Some pits can be very deep and/or pitted throughout the entire surface. These pieces will require much more time to get to a level of top quality.

Working the pits out can be time-consuming work. Determine what level of quality you want and just keep analyzing the pits and working on them until you are satisfied.

With some pieces, you will have one pit left, and you will want to remove it. You may sand it out and then buff it to perfection, only to find you hit a whole new set of pits. There will be imperfect metals within each piece that may not have mixed perfectly when the stainless was made. Different grades of stainless make a difference also. As you become more skilled at buffing, you will know when enough is enough and when diminishing returns will follow.

After you have learned the basics, you will want to move on to advanced sanding techniques. These include sanding at different angles, using special sanding pads to achieve a professional level. We will discuss using flap wheels and sandpaper, including using super fine grits by hand and scrutinizing the area for all imperfections in order to make each piece of trim better.

One option is using a die grinder with a flap wheel of 320

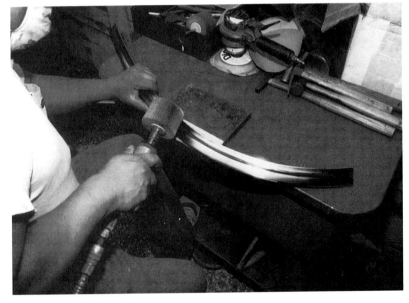

grit. These wheels are useful when smoothing imperfections in hard-to-reach areas which are not accessible for a DA sander. Also, the flexible wheel contours to many shapes. The outer edges of the flap wheel will reach the inside lines of a molding, while giving the operator maximum control.

Flap wheels are available from many companies that supply

This is a die grinder with a small flap wheel. It is useful for smoothing imperfections in hard-to-reach areas. The flexible wheel contours to many shapes, without leaving dips in the metal once it is polished. The best grits to use are 180-320.

51

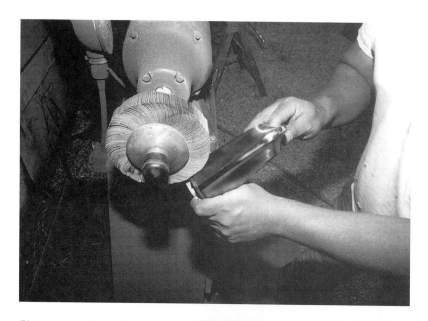

Another good way to remove imperfections is with a 6-inch flap wheel on your Baldor buffer. These are available in 80-320 grit sizes from the company. Flap wheels are very aggressive and fast when large like this, so check your work often. In order to be sure you like the results, as mentioned before, make tests on old parts.

After you have polished and buffed but still want to achieve even better finished results, sand by hand with 600 grit and 800 grit wet sandpaper in water

Pictured is a 6-inch flap wheel on a Baldor Buffer. This wheel is very aggressive and it removes imperfections very fast when used with 80-320 grit.

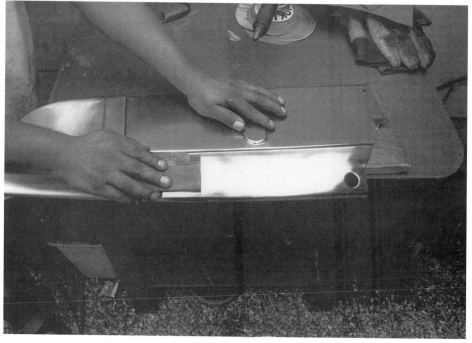

Super fine hand sanding stainless will help you to achieve a mirror finish. Using 600 and 800 grit wet paper with a small block works very well before the final buff.

machinery products. 3M also has a line of flap wheels. Note that there are many qualities of flap wheels. Inexpensive, lower quality flaps will not last long, whereas quality ones will have a long life. Like everything, you get what you pay for.

with a small block. This will make any small imperfections appear since you are grazing over the top surface with such a fine grade abrasive. When you polish this piece again, go straight to the KulKut buff and 812 compound which will be

52

Setup wheels are another way of removing imperfections quickly. The products you will need to make setup wheels include: glue, cloth wheels, various buffs, abrasive medium and a paint brush. Always buy these in kit form to assure compatible materials. These kits are from Tar Heel Products.

demonstrated in the next chapter and you will be amazed.

Some of you may use a sanding belt for larger items, but a setup wheel will work better on the hard-to-reach areas on smaller pieces. Here are the products you will need to make a set-up wheel:

TOOLS

1. Glue
2. Cloth wheels
3. Buffs of various contours and   sizes
4. Abrasive medium
5. Paint brush.

A setup wheel for your shop can be made right at home. A setup wheel consists of simplistic cloth type wheels with an abrasive grain bonded to them using glue. These products are all available through Tar Heel products and other companies.

It's recommended that beginners buy products in kit form. Purchase all the components in a kit, because they are matched to work best together. We recommend that you do not buy abrasives and glues separately, or you may get the wrong type.

According to how thick you want the wheel to be, take two or three of the cotton wheels and cover the sides with glue. Most smaller jobs only require the wheel to be 1/2 to 1-inch thick or wider

When making setup wheels, you begin by taking the number of cotton wheels you want and covering them with glue.

Once you have covered the wheels with glue, put them together with the glued sides touching. Make them as thick as you will need.

It is best to keep the wheels balanced during gluing. You can do this by finding something to fit into the wheel's arbor hole. This way, the wheels are even when put together.

Put glue around the outside edges evenly, so that the wheels don't get unbalanced.

for a particular application. Experiment to find the best results.

Now put the glued sides together. It is best to use a round object like a paint brush or round wooden stick that fits snugly in your wheels arbor hole. This will keep the wheels even, avoiding unbalanced wheels. Put the wheels together on the buffers shaft and let them dry this way preferably for four hours minimum.

Once the wheels are dried and bonded well, apply the glue to the outer edges. Be careful to get a smooth and even coat all the way around so that the wheel won't be unbalanced during the polishing process.

Now you want to roll the glue in the abrasive, pressing down on the wheel to cover it evenly with the abrasive grains. Try using a dish to ease in giving the wheel a medium coating. If you are mak-

ing a variety of wheels for the different grits such as 80, 120 and 180 mesh, make sure that the grits don't get mixed together. For cheap insurance against contamination mark the side of each wheel and abrasive container with which abrasive was used. Let the wheel dry for at least 24 hours. You may apply a second coating, but we do not recommend more than that.

Run the 8 to 10-inch wheel on a 3600 rpm Baldor for best results. As you begin to run your setup wheel, watch out! It will cut fast. We recommend that you test some old parts first to see the rate of cutting.

As your abrasives wear off and are not effective, soak the wheel in water, and run the wheel against an old file. They will then be ready for recoating.

Experiment with the wheel. You may find that you like to sand

You can make wheels with different size grits such as 80,120 and 180 mesh. Press the wheel with the glue on the outside down in the abrasive and slowly roll.

the imperfections of your parts with the wheel more than the DA method. Because of the flexibility of the wheel, you can do many things with a variety of angles. Most of all, the setup wheel will save you money compared to the DA sandpaper method. The DA sandpaper method only uses the edges of the paper, compared to the whole surface used with the setup wheel. The disadvantage is that the setup wheel will not plane the surface as true as the DA on flat surfaces. With this in mind, you may find yourself using both cutting styles on your parts for optimum results.

To run your setup wheels, it is best to use a Baldor 3600 RPM Buffer. The setup wheels will cut fast, so test and experiment with it on a rough, discarded piece of trim before working on your good pieces.

Another similar product you may prefer, due to its convenience of application, is Greaseless Compound available at Eastwood. These compounds are available in 80, 220, and 320 grit, and are used on either spiral-sewn or loose-section buffs to convert your buff into a flexible grinding wheel. The graded aluminum oxide abrasive in a water based cement is applied to a slowly spinning wheel, allowed to dry, and cracked for flexibility and fast cutting action.

CHAPTER FIVE

BUFFING TECHNIQUES

The buffing process is what makes the finished product. It is during this stage that all your hard work in tapping, pounding and sanding pays off.

Safety is a major concern while buffing. You will need a good face shield or goggles. We recommend a face shield, due to the nature of buffing. During the process, compounds fly off the wheels, making it a dirty process. A full face shield will keep your face clean—the goggles will not.

Gloves are a matter of choice. There are a few things to keep in mind when picking out appropriate gloves. Stainless holds a lot of high heat during the buffing process. You want a glove that can handle the heat, but still fits well for good grip. Gloves should also be soft enough to not scratch parts, especially during the final buff stages. At our shop, we use two different gloves—one for initial buff and another pair for final polish or coloring which has a very soft, cotton outer layer.

The main concern when purchasing a buffer is what you

If you are on a budget, you can buy a motor shaft adaptor like these from Eastwood and use an old washing machine or heater blower motor or remove the guards from your grinder, remove the grinding wheel and bolt on the buffing wheel.

A professional Baldor 333B is the best choice for buffing long pieces of trim. It has enough speed and power for big parts on any stainless project. A good source is The Eastwood Co.

want to do with the unit. If you are only going to polish a few small pieces, then an attachment for your bench grinder may suffice. If you are looking for a versatile machine, a good example is the combination Buffer/Grinder. If you want to do your whole car with long pieces of trim, then the Baldor 333B is needed. But if you plan on going into business full time doing a lot of trim restoration, then you may opt for a custom-made unit to change pulleys and belts for different speeds which is available from CF Global Product Systems Inc. As with anything, check prices on all comparable buffers to make the best purchase possible. Prices change all the time.

In the following text, we will discuss buffers, buffs and compounds as well as their different usage.

The Baldor buffer #333B has 3,600rpm, 3/4 horsepower, and enough speed and power with extended shafts for big parts on any stainless projects. This is available from Eastwood Company, Tar Heel Products and other suppliers.

There are several buffs necessary to achieve optimum results. Air Flow and Spiral Buffs are examples of types used to buff the trim. The sizes listed are common knowledge to any company selling buffs. Take the Spiral Sewn Sisal and place approximately three or four together. Placing several of these together should equal 3/8 Spiral Sewn Sisal, which provides adequate

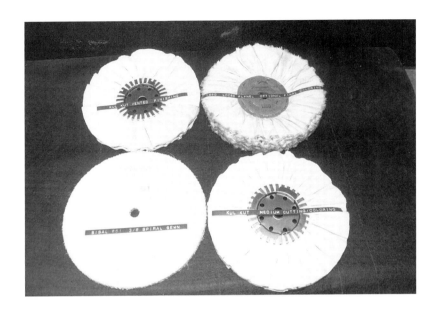

cutting and leaves a good finish. The 3/8 means that there is a sewn thread every 3/8 inch.

A faster cutting buff would come in the form of a 1/8 Spiral Sewn Sisal, which means there is only 1/8 of an inch between each circle of sewn thread, providing a much more stiff buff. This cuts quicker, but doesn't leave the texture quite as fine as the 3/8 sewn. Try them both, so you will be familiar with the different aspects of each and you will know which is best for your pieces. The KulKut buffs are medium buffs that take out small scratches and polish to a nice level.

A very important factor is the condition of the spiral sewn wheel at any given time. Our example shows a measurement of the distance across a slightly used spiral sewn buffing wheel. The buff has 8 1/2 inches, which will provide a surface speed of about 7,500 feet per minute. A new 10-inch buff would yield approximately 9,000 feet per minute which would be optimum.

Ventilated Flap Buffs and Spiral Buffs are used to buff the trim. Placing several together to obtain the desired thickness will provide the best results. A 3/8 spiral sewn means that there is 3/8 of an inch between each sewn thread on the buff. If you get a buff with more room, such as 1/2 inch between threads, it will be softer and less aggressive. The tighter the threads space is sewn, the stiffer the buff and the more aggressive it will be. You will need to experiment.

Sizing a spiral sewn buff's surface speed is determined by the diameter of the buff. An 8 1/2-inch buff will yield about 7,500 feet per minute on the Baldor.

A minimum of 7,000 feet per minute is ideal to efficiently cut and buff stainless steel trim. So, with the Baldor 3,600rpm buffer, I recommend not using buffs once they wear below the 8-inch mark, if you want to make good time. However, a beginner might like the 6- 7- or 8-inch wheels for slower working of metal, while getting used to what the buffs will do individually.

The buffs we used in this procedure are from CF Global Product Systems Inc., but other buffs of similar quality can be purchased from Tar Heel Products or Eastwood.

The Loose Section buff removes the fine hairline scratches that are left after using the previous Spiral Sewn buff, and it will polish out a piece of stainless to the completed stage if used properly. This buff is for polishing 320 and 400 sandpaper scratches and minor imperfections. It is currently 9-3/4 inches across. So, the

To clean your buffs, use a rake such as this one from Eastwood. Using a back and forth motion with 1-2 pounds of pressure will give you a good clean buff. Clean the wheel every 5-10 minutes and when you start up each day.

surface speed would be about 8,700 feet per minute and would yield excellent results in good time. Start with a new 10-inch buff for maximum results.

Your wheels will build up compound based on the amount of hand pressure you use. Clean your buffs when they have excess compound buildup and also before you begin each polishing session. Use a buffing rake to

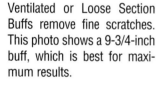

Ventilated or Loose Section Buffs remove fine scratches. This photo shows a 9-3/4-inch buff, which is best for maximum results.

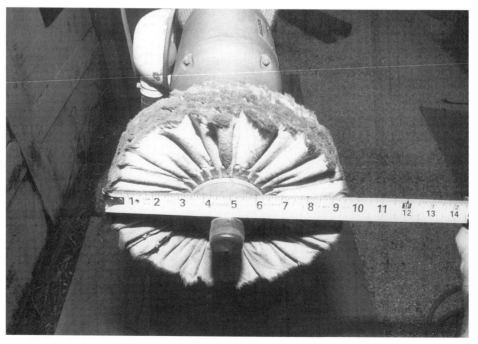

It is best to experiment with different compounds. Each type has a different effect on the stainless. Never mix compounds. Mark your buffs with which compound is used.

clean the wheels. These are available from Eastwood and others. Five seconds is all you need. Use a back-and-forth motion with 1 to 2 pounds of pressure.

You will want to experiment with different compounds. We have used three that we feel yield excellent results from CF Global Product Systems Inc.

For initial cutting on the Sisal Wheel use Emery compound; for medium to finish coloring and cutting use a Ventilated or Spiral Sewn wheel with Stainless. To finish up the coloring of the stainless to perfection, take a new Loose Section or cotton flannel and use white rouge compound.

Use a face shield as pictured during buffing to protect eyes and face. You can obtain this from Eastwood, Lab Safety, Northern Hydraulic or other companies.

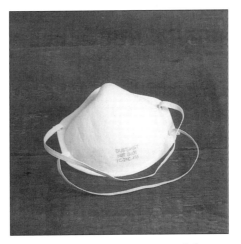

Protecting your respiratory system is important during buffing. Small particles formed by the compounds and buff wheels will be flying around.

Apply compound every 30 to 60 seconds of buffing for 3 second intervals. Your hand pressure during buffing will determine how much time your compound will last on the wheel and how effectively it will cut.

Use a face shield for eye protection and to keep face clean. You can find them at a variety of companies like Eastwood, Lab Safety Supply, Northern Hydraulic and others. Use a dust mask to keep from breathing dust particles formed by the compounds and buff wheels. And last but not least, wear gloves when polishing. Stainless steel holds heat like a hot coal, so gloves are a necessity. Thick leather gloves hold up well when roughing out parts in the first buffing stages. Use clean soft cotton gloves in the final finish polishing stages so the trim will not scratch.

Begin by applying the compound to the wheel—approximately every 30 to 60 seconds of buffing as a rule of thumb for 3 second intervals. Once again, experiment with how much time your compound lasts and cuts effectively. This will vary based on your individual hand pressure.

The side of the Sisal Wheel has "Emery" written on it to remind you that only Emery compound should ever be used on this wheel. Do not mix compounds together! Use only one type of compound on one wheel. Never let a wheel become mixed with different grades of compounds. For assurance, mark the wheel with a permanent marker as to which compound you are using on it.

The rubber plug covering the wheel attaching nut at the end of the shaft is necessary to protect your stainless piece if you should lose control of the piece during polishing.

Take note that there is a small pin stuck in the end of the bar of compound by the operators hand. We use different colored pins for each type of compound. Most compounds are identical in color and it is easy to mix them up and contaminate a wheel with another. Also, most compounds are not

62

It is important to hold the part correctly during the buffing process. Hold the piece with a slightly outstretched arm and rock your body when polishing.

marked with a reference number and can only be distinguished by smell once they become mixed up. So the colored pin method or your own way of keeping them separate is a necessity. Perhaps the individual smell of each compound will be your method, as they each definitely have their own unique odor.

There is a certain body form which is best for polishing. As the hubcap is being held with slightly outstretched arms, your body should rock to polish. This will be less fatiguing for a whole day of buffing. Always buff with the grain when buffing. This will ensure that the buffing wheel will not catch an edge and rip the piece out of your grasp, perhaps damaging or destroying the piece, or even worse, hurting yourself.

This is especially important around thin strip moldings like windshield and side trim. On odd

shaped pieces, try to buff lengthwise. Placing a board under long thin parts to help support them during buffing will make a big difference. In our example, the bottom of the hubcap is being buffed where contact is being made. If the top edge toward the worker's body was buffed, it would catch on the edge and perhaps rip the part from the worker's hands.

Make sure to angle the piece so that the buffing wheel doesn't catch an edge and rip the piece out of your grasp.

Small areas require small buffs using a die grinder. Tape the ends of your tools to keep them from scratching any areas they come in contact with.

Finish buff the edges. It is best to wear gloves during this step until you are very experienced. Always wear the gloves during high heat initial buffing stages.

On some small intricate areas, you may need to use a die grinder with an air regulator at approximately 45 psi to achieve best results, combined with a 4-inch buff from Eastwood. Be sure to tape the ends of your tools to keep them from scratching anything.

Mini buffs are available from Eastwood. These buffs are light when using a die grinder, but the regulator is very important when trying to get rpm down to about 4,000, compensating for the 4-inch buffs. Once again, experiment on old parts. Die grinders are available from most major tool companies.

Once you become more familiar and skilled, you can finish buff close areas such as edges with the large buff and not need gloves. Because you will have better hand control without gloves, you will be able to buff a line. However, use the gloves until you are very skilled. And always wear gloves during the high heat initial buffing stages.

After following the methods discussed, you will achieve excellent results. Our hubcap is now polished to perfection. Remember, it can take many hours to restore a piece. Be patient! The results are worth it.

Buffing Tips

When you are buffing extra long moldings, try taking a 1x4 board as long as your molding.

Pictured is a finished hubcap that has been buffed correctly. This is the level you want to achieve on your trim.

Lay the molding down flat on the board. Tape it down at one-foot sections. Buff between the tape. This will keep the molding from tearing out of your hands. Also, the board keeps the trim from warping. Remove the tape and place new tape on the area you buffed already and polish the hidden spots that were covered by the tape originally.

On small pieces like trim tags, door catches, and any small parts with small holes in them, take Philips head screws and screw the piece onto a 2x4 board. You can polish it without having it fly out of your grasp.

If you are going to buff the headlight retaining rings that hold the headlights on, it is best to take masking tape and run it over the tabs that stick out. This will help keep the buffer from catching on them and ripping the rings out of your hands.

Using a board to support long trim is the best thing to do to keep the pieces from warping, or worse yet, catching the buff and ripping out of your hands. Using tape at one foot intervals and buffing between the taped sections is the safest way to polish this type of piece.

Small pieces like trim tags, door catches and any piece with small holes in them
will be easier to work with if you screw them onto a board to polish them.

If you are working with headlight rings, or other pieces that have tabs that stick out, mask the tabs so that the buffer doesn't catch on them and tear the piece from your hand. The buffer is a powerful tool and must be respected.

CHAPTER SIX

REPAIRING AND WELDING

Many times it is hard to find a piece of trim to replace one that is torn or ripped. Instead, the piece you have will need to be repaired and have metal added to it for cosmetic or structural purposes. There may also be extra holes from screws where the trim was previously attached incorrectly.

In either case, you can repair the trim at home with just a few basic tools. You will want to straighten the piece with a few quick preparation steps, and then weld the piece back to hold its original shape. An 80 to 100 amp mig welder using stainless 024 wire and a special helium gas mixture are the basics. Of course, you will need some welding experience and some practice on an old piece of trim.

Be sure the part is clean (as specified in previous chapters) and has been inspected and marked for tears. Use a dolly to straighten the torn area by placing the dolly in an area that will support the flexible characteristics of the molding and tap the torn area in place. The damaged area should have only a small gap when shaped back to its original

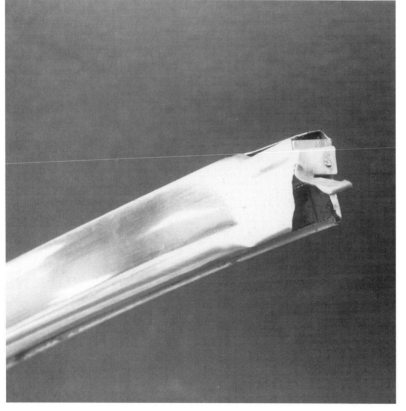

Once the stainless is cleaned, inspect it for tears. Once you have determined the type of damage, you will be able to select a method for repairing it.

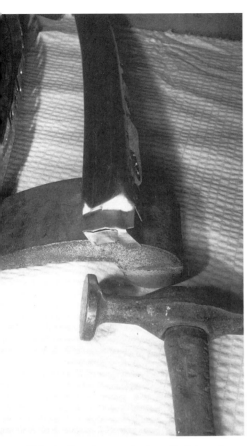

This is the damaged piece that has been reshaped into its original contour, so that there is only a small gap.

welding. This helmet allows excellent vision and maximum eye and face protection. Always keep your fire extinguisher near by, so you will have it when you need it.

You will need a welder with infinite heat control to be able to adjust the setting accordingly to make good welds. An excellent choice is the 88-amp, 110-volt MIG-Pak 10 from Eastwood. The proper gas mixture is 90 percent helium, 7.5 percent argon and 2.5 percent carbon dioxide for stainless welding. Now that you are ready to begin, take some time to study the welds. Most people know what a bad weld looks like. It is usually very uneven, with

contour. You may need to use a chisel or punch to get the molding back in shape. Do not weld until the piece is straight and fits your vehicle correctly. A pair of pliers can also be used to pull out mangled areas.

Four things you will need for welding are a good welding helmet, a mig welder, a damp towel and a fire extinguisher. It also helps to have a metal workbench or some sort of metal shield laying under the trim. You may even use a thick leather hide to keep the sparks off the wood on a wood workbench. We use a Hornell Speed Glass helmet for intricate jobs like stainless trim

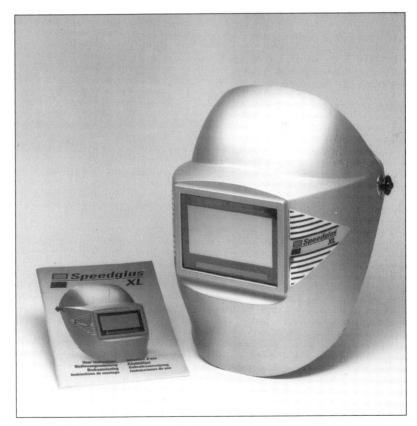

A Hornell Speed Glass helmet is the best eye and face protection to use with intricate stainless trim welding. This helmet provides excellent vision with maximum protection.

Pictured is a mig welder with .024 stainless wire in place. A good choice is a Century 105 amp 110 volt from A-I Supply with infinite heat control to adjust the settings.

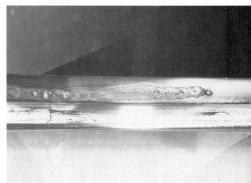

A bad weld will have a high buildup with irregular beads. Pictured is a model weld for which to strive.

The proper gas mixture is 90 percent helium, 7.5 percent argon and 2.5 percent carbon dioxide for stainless welding.

high buildup spots and irregular beads. Keep your mind focused on what you are trying to achieve. Take an old piece of stainless and practice with your technique until you can lay down good beads. A pulse technique consisting of pulling the trigger and releasing it, then pulling it again works best. Allow about 1 second between trigger pulls and then holding the trigger for 1 second.

If you have a Century welder, set your amps on 90, the wire speed on 5.5 and the heat range on 6. This will be a good starting point. How long you hold the trigger and how far you hold the welding torch will vary from one person to another and will alter the finished product.

The idea is to get the steel glowing red hot, then back off just for a split second. Then while the weld is still glowing, touch the trigger again, keeping it glowing without holding the trigger continuously. This gives the weld a chance to cool just a bit, but still melt together. And it aids in keeping the metal from burning through. This method provides excellent results.

On a molding that is wide and flat such as a rocker molding, use a damp rag to cool the

This shows a torn trim edge that has been welded correctly and is ready for the next step of grinding the weld down for a smooth finish.

weld every quarter of an inch or so to keep the metal from warping. Try placing the damp rag under the cracked area while welding.

Next, you will need to grind the weld down for a smooth finish. Take a hand-held grinder with 24 to 36 grit and grind the bead down to about a 1/32-inch thickness above the level of the original stainless, giving yourself some extra material to work with. The Ingersoll-Rand 302 Angle Grinder is excellent for this application. Also try the Mirka Trim Kut self-sharpening or Eastwood Flap Discs. Finish off the weld with an 80 grit disc.

In the chapter on sanding, we discussed the use of the DA, also known as Dual Action sander, the required tool for sanding out imperfections. The DA has both a grinding and an orbital mode. If you are good at using this tool, then you may want to finish the weld by grinding down with the DA sander set on the cutting mode. Use 80 grit and smooth down to the original thickness. Be very careful not to smooth down through the original thickness or you will have to start over again. It is better to leave the piece a little extra thick then to grind through and leave it brittle. Keep practicing on some old parts until you have perfected the process before welding your important pieces of stainless.

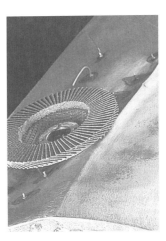

The cool running Flap Discs from Eastwood feature a beveled surface for long life and controllability.

After grinding the welds down and following all the sanding steps, you can finish off the weld with an 80 grit disc.

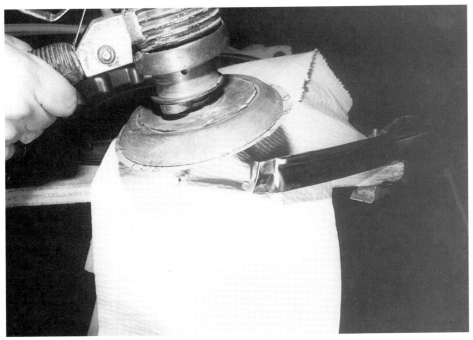

Smooth down close to the original thickness, using a DA sander with 80-180 grit paper. It is better to leave it a little thicker than to grind through and start over.

CHAPTER SEVEN

WORKING WITH ALUMINUM

Aluminum is a softer metal than stainless, so be careful because it will straighten, buff and polish faster. Be extremely careful that you do not sand or buff it too thin. You will use the same basic techniques as in stainless restoration, but it will only take a third of the time. Pits in aluminum will appear small, but during the process of sanding and buffing, you will quickly learn that pits sometimes go all the way through the thickness of the metal. So, you will need to learn what to look for while analyzing aluminum trim. Many times, because of the pitting, you will want to replace the pieces when they are prominent. But unlike stainless trim, aluminum deteriorates at a much faster pace, thus making it more difficult to find good pieces to start with.

As a rule of thumb you must be even more careful when straightening this type of trim. Here are some tips to follow:

STEPS

1. Pry only 1/3 the amount during removal and straightening compared to stainless restoration.
2. Tap half as hard.
3. Use finer grit when sanding. It is suggested to use nothing under 180 grit for aluminum, to ensure you don't destroy the pieces by over sanding.

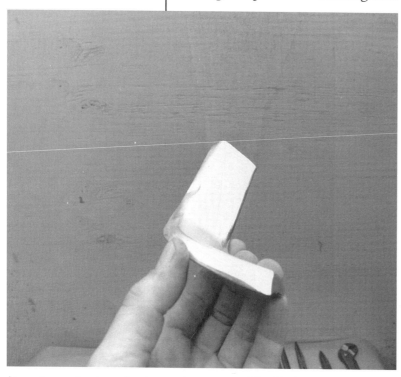

Inspect your aluminum for damaged areas as explained in Chapter 2.

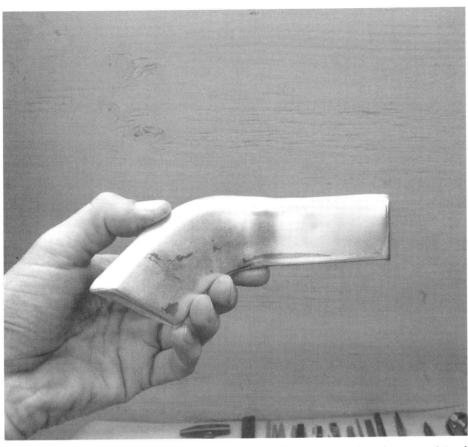

A different view reveals other damage, so be sure and inspect your piece from a variety of angles. Mark them as explained, using a permanent black marker.

Polishing will take less time. And because of the finer grits of sandpaper, it will not take as long when polishing the parts out. When you are finished with the polishing stages of aluminum, there are three steps you could take to increase longevity, since aluminum does not hold up as well to the environment as stainless:

STEPS

1. **Re-brite dip, for original condition for concours showing**
2. **Clear coat to ward off oxidation**
3. **Anodize Recolor for special applications.**

To start, you will need to inspect your aluminum pieces. During inspection, you will notice flaws. Remember the more different shapes and sizes you encounter or familiarize yourself with, the better you will be able to straighten, buff and polish the pieces.

Our example shows a different angle of the dip in the center of the piece. It will need to be removed. Begin with the edge. Because of the rounded shape, you must use a pair of pliers with 1/4-inch thickness in the jaws or less when prying back the edge. Pulling back an edge is only necessary when the damage is close to an edge and you cannot tap it out from the backside.

If the damage is close to an edge and cannot be tapped out from the backside, pry back the edge with 1/4-inch wide pliers until it stands up in the area that is damaged. Be careful! Aluminum is very fragile compared to stainless.

Slowly but surely, pry back the edge until it stands straight up in the area that is damaged. Aluminum bends easily, so use caution. Take a 1/4-inch-wide chisel with a slightly dulled edge. This will insure you do not make the edge too sharp when tapping back the original shape. Start on one end and work your way down until you have covered the entire length of damage. Tap gently, for aluminum is a soft metal and it moves easy. Take a small hammer and gently tap out the flat area evenly, being very careful. Use a 1x4 board to support the piece. This permits the metal to be stretched very effectively but it still supports it evenly.

As noted in the stainless section of the straightening chapter, use your permanent marker and color the damaged area. Sand the area and see where your low spots are. Then take a small punch and tap out any small areas that may need attention. Use the marker again, sand it with 220 grit and check for low spots. This will tell you where you need more tapping. On the very back edge you will be able to see the low spots that come from using the marker technique. Go back and tap these low areas very slowly.

You may need to use a vise on some pieces. You may encounter a molding has a very sharp dent or is structurally bent on its longest end. For this type of

Aluminum bends very easily so be careful when you tap on it. Tap very easily or you may damage it.

This photo demonstrates small Hammer tapping gently so as not to mar the aluminum which is a very soft metal and can be damaged easily. Approximately half the pressure needs to be applied compared to stainless trim.

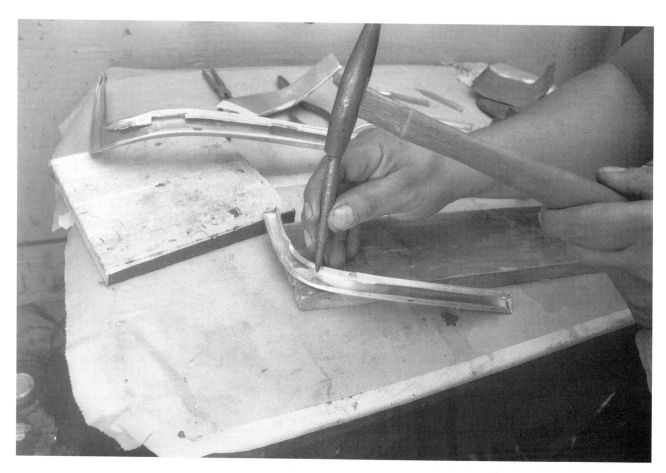

A small punch is used for light tapping on the soft aluminum. Move your punches and chisel approximately half the distance between each tap as compared to the requirements for stainless. Once again, use caution and tap very gently.

If you color in the flaws with a black permanent marker and then sand it with 220 grit, any marker left over will indicate low areas that you will need to tap out further. Sanding is a much safer way to find the areas that need more tapping and then filing on the softer material aluminum.

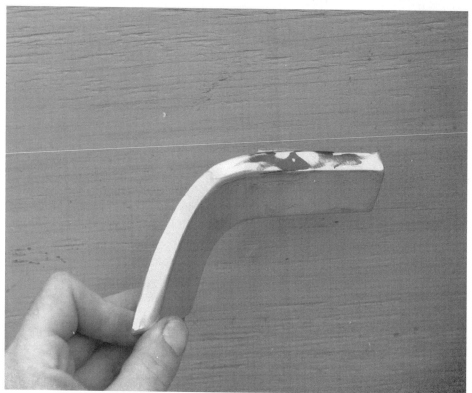

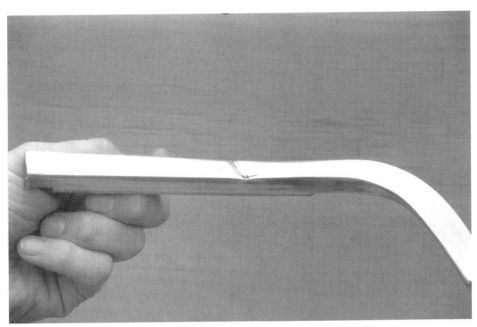

Analyze the type of damage done on the molding. For example, use a vise for straightening a sharp dent or a molding that is structurally bent in order to hold the part stiff. Always use cardboard or rubber jaws in the vise for protection.

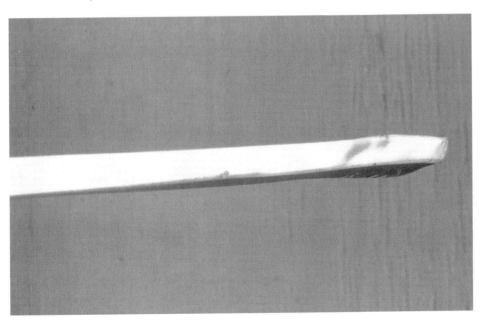

damage, place the backside edge in a vise and follow the methods described. The main emphasis at first, is to get the molding to fit the body panels right and make even contact over the whole area.

Before any dents are straightened in the center, always get the outer edges to fit the body panels evenly first. If there is a dent in the center of the molding, the edges or paint contact points will be inaccurate, so they need to be fixed first. Pry up slightly, so as not to bend too much at a time. How much you pry and with what amount of pressure and

Pry up slightly with the vise and keep in mind that the aluminum is soft and pliable and will move quickly and easily.

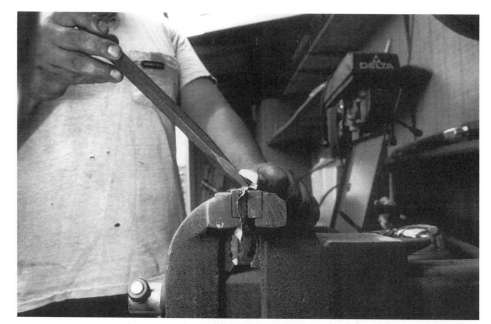

Once you have taped thin cardboard to the jaws of the vise or used rubber or aluminum jaws, you can place the trim in the vise at different angles, then pry.

As demonstrated, you must squeeze back the edges of the aluminum to straighten the areas that have dips.

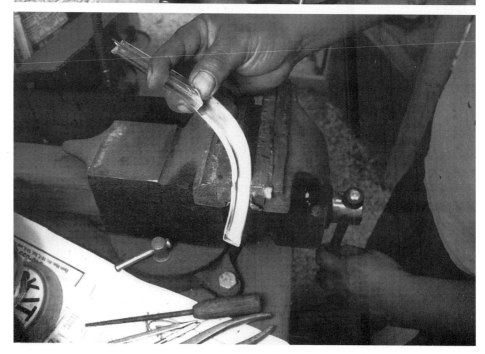

Pliers help pull back the edge again on straight trim to gain access to the damage. In tight areas you may have to use 1/4- 1/2- 5/8 wide pliers, or somewhere in between, to pull back an edge. You do not want to twist and mangle up the surrounding metal when pulling back an edge.

Use a sharp pointed chisel with the technique described in the text to bring out the ridge again in a fine line. The biggest concern is to fit the size line with the same shaped chisel, be it a sharp, thinly ground tip or a thick, dull tip.

Using a wide chisel to achieve a nice ridge line is something you may try in your decision on the correct size fit for your trim. You may also want to grind different tips to custom tailor your trim repair needs.

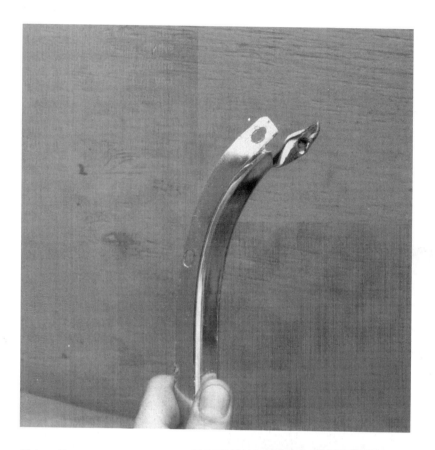

leverage will determine how you will achieve optimum results. Just remember you are now dealing with aluminum, which is a very soft and easily moved metal.

Place the edges in the vise and tighten it slightly inward to get the correct size. Use smooth rubber jaws, aluminum jaws or thin cardboard taped to the jaws, so there will be no teeth marks. You may also have to squeeze back the edges to straighten some of the areas that have dips. To help shape the original piece which is very contoured, lay a thin sheet of cardboard under the trim. Again tap very lightly.

In our example we used pliers to pull back the edge to gain access. Next the ridge (which appears from the front side to be a crisp line)

Pictured is an example of a torn piece of trim which will need to be repaired. Aluminum trim is often weaker than the clips that hold it on. Therefore, when an object catches it, the aluminum will tear instead of the clip shearing from the body.

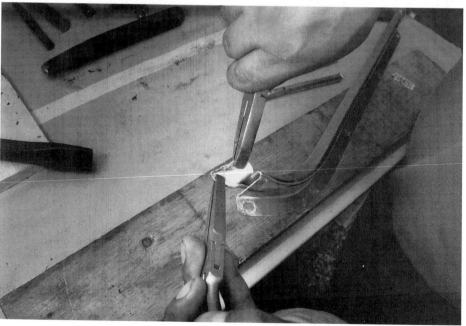

When aluminum becomes torn, simply use pliers to bend the torn pieces back into shape easily. The correct angle of bending the pieces back into shape comes with experience. Damage is usually different, requiring a unique approach with each piece.

When working on a torn piece of trim, you can reshape the end with a chisel by tapping the edge flat and then bending it back out of its original shape.

needs to be brought out. Back the piece with a 1x4 piece of wood, tapping lightly right in the seam and moving a quarter inch at a time. You can use different size chisels to achieve the line needed for each piece of trim as you become more familiar with the process.

Aluminum metal usually tears when struck by an object from the side or when the edge of the trim is caught. Sometimes the screw or clip holding the trim down is stronger than the trim itself, which aids in the soft metal tearing.

To repair this type of damage, take a couple of 1/4-inch wide pli-

ers and start to bend it back into shape. Be careful. As with any metal, the more you bend it back and forth, the sooner it will weaken and break off. This would be very hard to do on stainless, but soft aluminum allows for easy straightening. Take a chisel and reshape the small edge on the tip or end of the trim, tapping it flat as it was originally, and then bending it back to its original shape. Have a friend or coworker hold the piece upright and tap the contour to the original shape. A small piece of angle iron or similar metal acts as the perfect anvil to straighten a small tip. Use the appropriate

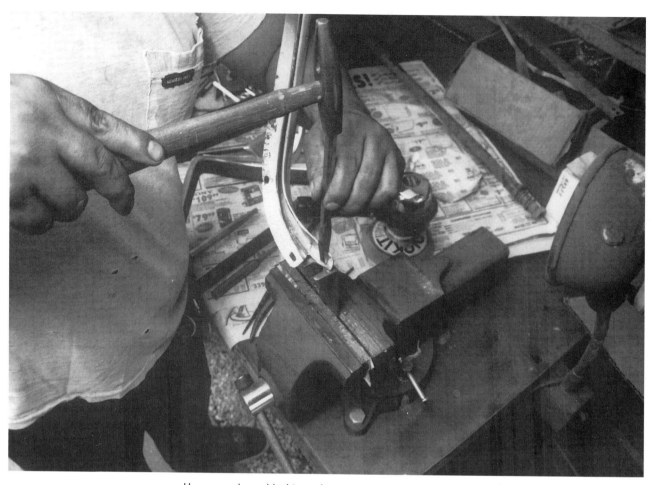

Use a punch or chisel to reshape grooves on your piece of trim as close to the original shape as you can.

punch or chisel to force the correct shape back into place.

Finish it off with a small hammer, then proceed to the welding steps. For aluminum, the welding is the same as for the stainless, except that you use an aluminum wire and the appropriate gas mixture. The weld will grind down much faster than stainless. Of course, you will have to dial in your heat settings for your particular abilities. Last but not

least, the welding procedure requires a different gas mixture of 100 percent argon for welding aluminum. Remember to use aluminum wire. Experiment with the welding techniques on old trim first until you become skilled enough to perform this procedure correctly.

You can use a thick and wide blade chisel to tap out a door molding that is basically flat. Remember to get the part

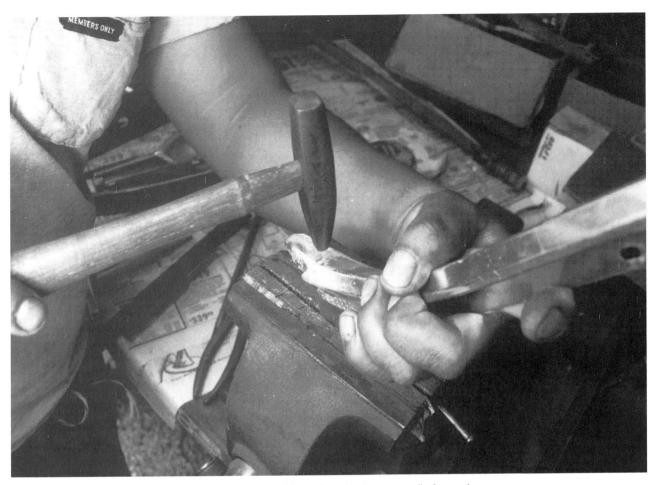

Finish off the edge with a small hammer, lightly tapping it into place, leaving as small of a crack as possible. Then proceed to welding. Using an aluminum mig or hel arc is best.

straight on the outside edges first. This allows the damaged areas in the center of the metal to have room to move.

Be sure and use the same sanding and polishing techniques as outlined earlier in the stainless sections. Just remember that aluminum sands and polishes much faster.

The only real differences in stainless and aluminum is oxidation, which comes in the form of pits. These pits can destroy the metal and make it impossible to polish out to perfection, so choose your aluminum trim carefully. Also, the metal is softer and requires much less pressure when prying or tapping to straighten. Polishing will also be performed at a faster rate. Never go below 180 grit when sanding out imperfections or it may cut too thin, too fast. Also, finish off aluminum with 400 grit before polishing.

ABOVE AND RIGHT: Use a thick wide chisel to tap out door moldings that are straight and flat. Start on the outside lines first, then work the middle. The chisel should be ground smooth and straight across the tip.

CHAPTER EIGHT

DIECAST, CHROME, COPPER AND NICKEL

For pre-paint cleanup use Pre-Kleano by R and M Automotive to remove compound, tar, fingerprints and silicone residue. This is a wax and grease remover that works well on this type of trim, and will eliminate any fish-eye contamination during the painting process.

Painting on any type of trim, stainless and aluminum has three requirements:

1. Straighten and polish the part to your liking first and foremost.

2. Decide what areas you want to be painted. They are to be masked off to keep paint off any areas that are to remain polished metal.

3. Use the right primer for maximum adhesion. This will give you the longevity you desire.

Here are the recommended steps for painting trim:

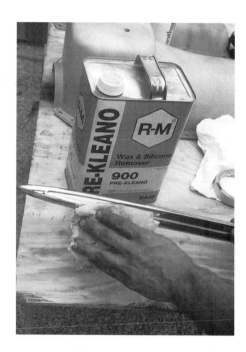

STEPS

1. After the trim is polished to your satisfaction, clean up the molding with "Pre-Kleano" wax and grease remover by R and M or a comparable brand. This takes off any compound and oil residue avoiding silicone during painting.

2. Tape off the area of the molding that you don't want to get paint on 3M tape is best.

3. When you finish taping it off, take a micro fine scuff pad by Norton or 3M and lightly rub over the area you will paint. Do this with a straight stroke to leave straight super fine lines on the area and avoid lifting up the tape edge you just laid down.

4. Take DP 90 Epoxy Primer and 402 Catalyst from Ditzler. Mix half and half. Spray on one light coat. This will stick to the metal well and give you the adhesion you need.

5. Decide on what shade of color the insert should be. Take your paint and spray over the top of the DP 90 after it has sat for one hour. We used Krylon, the correct gold shade that was needed. Usually painted moldings have white, black or gold in the center. You can pick the type of paint you like, but enamels and urethanes last longest. Let sit for 5-10 minutes. Then peel back the tape away from the painted insert to avoid peeling off the paint.

When you are going to paint inserts, use masking tape to tape off the area you don't want painted.

Scuff the area that is masked off with a micro fine scuff pad by 3M. Scuff with a straight stroke to leave straight, fine lines.

Before painting, prime the piece with DP 90 Epoxy Primer and 402 Catalyst. This will stick to the metal and give you good adhesion for your paint.

Choose the color you want your insert to be and then use Krylon or similar paint. Be sure and let the Epoxy DP 90 sit and cure for at least one hour and no more than 24 hours before you paint.

When it is time to prepare your steel and diecast part for plating copper, nickel and chrome, you need to have the pieces stripped of all three platings first by an expert. Look in Hemmings Motor News for the nearest place or the Yellow Pages for a local source.

Don't even attempt to strip the copper, nickel or chrome on your own. The chemicals that are used are toxic and it is against the law to utilize these on your property due to the disposal problem. In addition, timing is so important or parts can be damaged beyond repair. Many pieces may have uneven layers of plating on them, especially around the edges where buildup during the immersion process took place.

Before sending it out, you can make the biggest difference in the quality of each bumper or trim piece by doing the following:

STEPS

1. Fit the bumper or trim piece to the vehicle.
2. Determine if you are satisfied with the gaps between the vehicle's body and trim.
3. If you are not satisfied, use the Hustler stick from ALC to align bumper gaps to vehicle, and diecast parts can have the edges trimmed and sanded to fit better.

A hood center bar of a 1957 Chevrolet needed sanding before replating. The chrome was removed. Then we sprayed black Krylon so highs and lows would show up during the sanding procedures.

Steel in a bumper is very thick, ranging from 1/16- to 1/8-inch, which means it can be worked with a lot. Think of a bumper as you would the body of the vehicle. Everyone wants a straight body and nice paint. The same can be achieved with a bumper. Every ripple or dent can be taken out and made to fit perfectly, if you are willing to put the time into the project.

Once the pieces have been electro-chemically stripped, and the backsides sand blasted, the base metal needs to be ground, sanded, polished and buffed to remove any irregularities, pits, or scratches. The reason this is so important is that none of the three layers—copper, nickel, or chrome—are capable of filling these areas or covering them. Copper may work into some of the small pits, but in the long run, the best plating you can have begins with the best preparation of the base metal.

At the plating shop you will want to make sure they understand the value of your classic vehicle. Get a guarantee that

they will take the proper amount of steps in grinding and polishing. Copper, nickel and chrome won't hide many flaws if the steel or diecast metals are not worked out first.

Pot metal is a conglomeration of all types of cheap metals mixed together. Deep cavities, bubbles, pits, and corrosion can be present on these pieces. You can purchase some of these trim items reproduced, but the same type of flaws may be present in the castings. The pot metal needs to be sanded down to remove some of the trouble spots. Some shops will use silver solder to fix deep pits on other pieces, but in general pot metal is the hardest, most inconsistent to work with.

Once you have achieved a smooth surface on the base material, follow with the three layer step of applying copper, nickel and chrome at your chrome shop. You can fill pits with silver solder or drill out each pit with a drill bit. Then using a tap set, thread a fine thread hole and screw brass plugs into each, then grind/polish smooth. Even though most people will never attempt to do this at home, it is a good idea to understand the process so you know what to expect when hiring a company to do it.

Each coating has a special reason for its use. For example, copper is used for adhesion between the base metal and nickel. It is also used like a primer since it fills minor imperfections. It must be sanded with finer grits each coating. Nickel is for brightness and minor filling and chrome is a

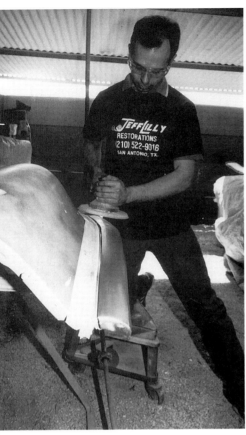

"Pre-chrome" preparation. After the chrome has been stripped off at a chrome shop, you can sand diecast or pot metal parts like this by using power and hand tools to take out imperfections, much like the body of a car. Sand the part with a sanding block, preferably 8 to 18 inches long. Work out a few bad spots with a DA if needed. You will see copper and nicklel undercoats as you slice down the part to make it even. Periodically check the part for thickness to make sure it isn't cut too thin. Keep it a minimum of 1/16 inch.

sealant or protectorate and final plating treatment. There are different methods used to apply all of these.

Applying Copper

Copper can be worked into low spots because of its pliable make-up. It will bond with automotive base metals and can be polished up nicely. You can use it to build up a surface by layering copper and nickel. Acid copper is the highest built copper available. Copper also protects against any future corrosion to the metal. Essentially, copper is the best choice to have under your nickel and your chrome.

Parts will need to be immersed in the copper tank for 20 minutes or more. Then level, grind and recoat. Take your bumper or trim and sand down the copper with 220 or 320 grit. Stop when you hit base metal. Have it copper plated again. Watch the edges, since the copper will build up fastest here. Next sand with 600 to 800 grit, working up to 1000 grit, blocking out imperfections each time.

Many of the irregularities in pot metal won't even show up at first until you have begun the copper process. Then it may take many layers of copper to cover these areas. Again, copper will not fill the pits, but can be worked in and built up. It needs to be sanded or polished between each plating. Make sure that your pieces aren't warped from the polishing process. If there was any engraving on your parts removed during the buffing process, now is the time to have it replaced, since copper is soft enough to have the engraving done.

Applying Nickel

Nickel is much more difficult to work with than copper. It will cover some pits and scratches, unlike chrome, but once again, it is the base metal preparation and the copper that do the real work. In addition, nickel doesn't polish as nicely as copper does either.

But many parts were plated with nickel, so it may be necessary to use it, without chroming over the top of it. Nickel was the best plating used until chrome platings were discovered.

Parts can be in the nickel tank from 75 minutes to 2 hours. Once it is finished, it needs to be buffed. If any of your pieces look like they have gold plating, it is more likely to be brass plating over the copper and nickel. This is a troublesome type of plating because it requires continual polishing also.

Applying Chrome

For show quality work, you won't want to build up many layers of chrome. Remember it is not the chrome that provides the smooth surface, but the properly prepared base metal and plating of copper and nickel, as well as polishing that makes the difference.

Parts are carefully immersed in the chrome tank for up to three minutes. It will form a blue hue over the nickel. Work the base metal for nice, wave-free parts.

If you have a good trim piece that fits the car well, take it to a stripping company and have them remove the chrome and nickel. Leave the copper on if

Large board files such as a Hutchins Hustler Board File with 80 grit paper evens out flaws quickly. Change the paper often, because pot metal will dull the paper and load up fast.

the part is crater-free, because you can sand it off easily and it will act as a high or low indicator for you.

Our example is the hood center bar of a 1957 Chevrolet that has been stripped. When the length of the piece was inspected, it was found to have a lot of ripples in it, so it needed to be sanded down. Dark copper spots indicate low areas. If the copper has already been stripped off, then spray the piece with black epoxy primer. Block sand it to find the high or low areas. Black Krylon will also work.

To be sure of an even height fit at the hood, and also to be able to sand without touching the hood, use washers wrapped in tape. Place them behind the hood bar to stick out about a 1/4 inch between the hood and the hood bar. Also, put tape on the body's primed surface so that if the sander jumps over it, nothing will be ruined. With an 80 grit high speed DA sander, you can even it out quickly, as you file down the high spots. Use a long board file such as the Hutchins Hustler Board File or a similar type and sand the piece lengthwise, just like you would do on the side of a quarter panel. Use 80 grit paper and change it often, as it gets worn down or loads up with the soft diecast metal. Take a 17-inch hand block by 3M and block sand in a criss-cross pattern until you don't see any more of the black primer or the copper spots. Remember to use the 80 grit, 180 and 400. The piece is ready to be re-plated with copper. Sand it with 800-1000 grit. Then polish the copper and apply the nickel

and chrome plate to highlight the beauty.

When you are done with the trim and satisfied, take clean newspaper and wrap it around the pieces and tape it. This is the best way to store the trim in order to avoid scratches until assembly time.

Hand block sand with a 17-inch hand block by 3M in a criss-cross pattern to finish getting rid of highs and low spots in 80 grit. Finish off the part with 180 then 320 before giving back to your plater for re-chroming.

Once your trim is completed, you will want to take special care to store it where it won't get any damage while you are finishing up the restoration of your vehicle. Wrap it in clean newspaper and tape it so that it doesn't get any scratches.

CHEMICAL AND PARTS DISPOSAL

One of the real problems of doing your own restoration is what to do with the junk and poisonous fluids you inevitably generate. Everybody knows these days that two of our largest environmental problems are the related ills of landfill overuse and groundwater contamination. Unfortunately, our interest in environmental problems far outstrips our ability to find answers to them right now.

Some areas have remarkably advanced programs for disposal of hazardous waste, but most locales don't. Your first step in being a responsible garbage maker is to do some of your own research. The city or county listings in your telephone blue pages will have an entry for Waste Disposal, Hazardous Waste Management or something similar. Don't expect to get many answers the first time–it can be a real trick to finally find the right outfit since there are still no uniform rules across the country for waste management.

There are, however, hazardous waste disposal sites and procedures for every location–it just may be one heck of a long way off, and your local government may not have heard about it yet. If you come across a situation like this, it'll be your ironic duty to find the answers yourself and educate your leaders.

If you strike out with the government at first, call around to local garages, body shops, and restoration specialists; they're required by law to dispose of toxics in an organized manner, so they should be helpful.

Disposal of Chemicals

The best rule of thumb as you work with chemicals and fluids is to remember that if you can smell it, it's bad news. And the stronger the odor the more dangerous it is, both to your immediate health and to the atmosphere and water table. Cleaners, paints, and all oil-derived liquids are the big things to watch out for. Dumped carelessly by the wayside, these toxic chemicals will quickly enter the water cycle and come back to haunt everybody.

The easiest solution, of course, is not to make any more of these wastes than necessary in the first place. Except for motor oil, the greatest volume of volatiles is generated by cleaning. It's best to start off with the mildest cleaners possible at first–soap and water can, in fact, do a lot of work–not just for the environment's sake but because these are also the easiest on the part itself.

You'll inevitably generate some hazardous materials no matter what you do, however. Things like spray cleaners and naphtha, for example–real health and environmental nightmares–are just too convenient to realistically swear off completely. The trick is simply to catch as much of these fluids as possible after use, and to keep them tightly covered in glass or metal containers until you can safely get rid of them. Leaving pans of cleaners uncovered sends these toxins directly into the atmosphere through evaporation, so keep them covered, always.

Caked grease and ruined rags should also be kept tightly wrapped up in a cool place and disposed of along with actual fluids–they're simply volatiles that are currently trapped in solid form.

All toxics should be kept separated since cross contamination simply makes the disposal issue harder. Motor oil, for example, can actually be recycled and used as fuel for ships and other things. If it's contaminated with minute traces of brake fluid, though, the entire batch in the collection tank will be ruined.

Disposal of Parts

Actual pieces of mechanical junk are generally more of a pain than a danger to dispose of, assuming that the pieces aren't filled with fluid or that particularly greasy, metal parts will sit happily inert in a landfill and actually decompose over time, albeit often a long time. If possible, you should bring big metal parts to a local junkyard; often yards will accept these pieces and use them for their scrap value. Smaller metal pieces, well, there's not much more you can do than to throw them away. The residual Grease and oil won't make the local dump an ideal whooping crane nesting site, but at this point in time there aren't a lot of alternatives.

The same goes for plastic and small rubber parts, which actually do release a number of carcinogenic chemicals as, or if, they decompose. Again, though, until a coherent method of disposal is hit on, you don't have a lot of choice here but to throw them out.

Tires, on the other hand, are so well known, as a dumping hazard that standards and methods for their disposal have been developed. Generally, the response has simply been to tell people that they can't dump their tires here–which ultimately is the wrong answer, since many people just get frustrated and toss them by the side of the road or in a vacant lot.

A relatively recent and common development are mandatory tire buyback laws; some areas have regulations that force tire dealers to accept used tires for disposal, usually with a small fee attached. Though there's no really good way for the dealer to get rid of the tires either, at least the problem is narrowed down to one source instead many. Look into it.

Since regulatory agencies are currently for behind the scale of the waste problem, something else I encourage you to do is start making some noise about getting a comprehensive disposal plan developed for your city or county. Grass-roots organizations have formed in most places to look at the issue, and automotive and truck enthusiasts need to be involved. We're the ones making a lot of the problems, so we'll need to be the ones helping to sort them.

SUPPLIERS

A/T Supply, 401 Radio City Drive, North Pekin, IL 61554, 1-800-553-5592

C.F. Global Systems, 1304 Sunset Avenue, Yorkville, IL 60560, 1-800-333-2833

Channel Lock, 1306 South Main Street, Meadville, PA 16335, (814) 724-8700

Ditzler, 19699 Progress Drive, Strongsville, OH 44136, 1-800-245-2590

Eastwood Co., 580 Lancaster Avenue, Malvern, PA 19355-0714, 1-800-345-1178

Hornell Speed Glass, 2374 Edison Boulevard, Twinsburg, OH 44087, 1-800 234-5688

Hutchins, 49 North Lotus Avenue, Pasedena, CA 91107, (817) 792-8281

Ingersol-Rand, 510 Hester Drive, Whitehouse, TN 37188, (615) 672-0321

Lab Safety, 401 South Wright Road, Janesville, WI 53546, 1-800-356-0783

Mirka Abrasives, 7950 Bavaria Road, Twinsburg, OH 44087, 1-800-843-3904

National Detroit, 1590 North Rock Court, Rockford, IL 61103, (815) 877-4041

Northern Hydraulics, P.O. Box 1219, Burnsville, MN 55337, 1-800-222-5381

SK Tools, 3535 West 47th Street, Chicago, IL 60632, (312) 532-1300

S and H Industries, 5200 Richmond Road, Bedford Heights, OH 44146, 1-800-253-9726

Tar Heel Products, P.O. Box 2604, Matthews, NC 28106-2604, 1-800-322-1957

Urethane Supply, 264 Kirk Road Southwest, Rainsville, AL 35986, 1-800-633-3047

Vise Grip Tools, 108 South Pear Street, Dewitt, NE 68341, 1-800-228-4204

INDEX